D1277399

THE ONE HOUR ORGASM

HOW TO HAVE MORE FUN BY INTENSIFYING & LENGTHENING THE ORGASMIC STATE FOR YOURSELF AND YOUR PARTNER

And Other Information To Make Your Relationship Work Better

by Bob Schwartz

Author of the New York Times Best Seller,
DIETS DON'T WORK

Based On Personal Experience Using The Teachings
Of Dr. W. Victor Baranco, Ph.D.

Copyright 1988, Robert M. Schwartz

Breakthru Publishing

THE ONE HOUR ORGASM

COPYRIGHT © 1988 BY ROBERT M. SCHWARTZ

ISBN 0-942540-03-4

1 2 3 4 5 6 7 8 9 10/94 93 92 91 90 89 88

All rights reserved. No part of this book may be reproduced in whole or in part in a retrieval system or transmitted in any form by an electronic, mechanical, photocopying, recording means or otherwise, without permission in writing from the author.

Published by
BREAKTHRU PUBLISHING
P.O. Box 2866
Houston, Texas 77252-2866
Phone (713) 529-4153

Printed in the United States of America

ACKNOWLEDGMENTS

I wish to thank Dr. W. Victor Baranco, Ph.D., of More University, and his staff for their dedication and integrity while working with my wife, Leah, and I to help us write this book.

And to Leah, the love of my life. Without your help this book would not have been written. Thank you for sticking by me for the last ten years and teaching me how to love someone with all my heart. I promise to spend the rest of my life giving you whatever you want, whenever you want it, for as long as you want it.

AUTHOR'S NOTE

Reading this book can feel like you are riding a roller coaster. You may feel happy one paragraph and angry the next. You could disagree with an idea in one chapter and then find yourself starting to agree with the same idea later on.

Keep an open mind until you have read the whole book. Follow the instructions and have fun.

The purpose of this book is entertainment. *THE ONE HOUR ORGASM* will also increase the amount of joy, pleasure, and productivity in your life.

TABLE OF CONTENTS

———————————•———————————

———————————•———————————

TABLE OF CONTENTS

TABLE OF CONTENTS

TABLE OF CONTENTS

Master The Possibilities
Over The Top
Doing Your Man
Women's Positions
Picture of the Penis Area
Over The Top

Editor . . . . Frank Reuter
Typesetting . . . . J. Jones Word Merchant

Chapter 1

WHAT'S IN THE WAY?

———————————————•———————————————

"Is this a joke?", asked a friend when I told him what I was working on.

No. This is a book that I have tried to talk myself out of writing for over three months now. The material about to be presented to you has shaken the very roots of my life and my already successful relationship with my wife. If it could make such a positive difference in our lives, how could I not share the value with others?

The value of this book goes far beyond the promise of the title. When I first heard of Dr. W. Victor Baranco's work about sex, female pleasure, and relationships, I was not interested. Our sex life was

———————————————•———————————————

better than good—it was one of the best parts of our relationship. Then, some of my weight loss clients who had begun to study Dr. Baranco's work began to rapidly reach their personal and weight goals. I became interested. What finally hooked me was that some of the people who had studied Dr. Baranco's teachings had lost as much as 100 pounds without dieting.

It had taken me twenty-four years of study and research to write and publish my first book, *DIETS DON'T WORK*, which teaches people with eating disorders and weight problems how to lose weight. Yet here was some guy teaching people how to sex better, and some of them were losing weight without even reading my book.

I did not like the idea of going to a "sex" course. Someone might think my wife and I needed help. On the other hand, a lot of people I respected, plus thousands of others, had studied Dr. Baranco's work at More University in Northern California, and they seemed to get a great deal of value out of it. What did I have to lose?

Without knowing it at the time, I had begun. I had already discovered one of, what we will describe in chapter 4 as, my "DON'TS". "DON'T LET ANYONE THINK THAT THERE IS ANYTHING YOU DON'T KNOW ABOUT GREAT SEXING."

THE SECRET WORD: "TUMESCENCE"
(TU-MESS-ENCE)

The first new thing I learned is that women have heat cycles. "So what?" I thought to myself, not realizing that female heat cycles are a source of enormous power. It is a power that needs to be understood and mastered in order to have relationships and sexual experiences beyond our present reality.

O.K., O.K.. My wife and all other women have monthly cycles and even yearly cycles. I knew that! (I think.)

I had noticed that one of the main reasons I married my wife, Leah, was that she was so "nice." Leah was the first person who read my book, *DIETS DON'T WORK*. By applying the principles in the book, her weight declined from 175 to 135 pounds over the next 3 months without dieting. It was at that moment that I fell in love with her. Anyone who finds everything you do to be right and is so very nice is not a person you want to let out of your sight. So, we got married.

After that, especially around the time of her periods, I began to notice that my wife got slightly meaner and meaner as each month passed. The longer we were married, the meaner she seemed to get. No matter what I came up with to soothe her, I always felt something was missing.

I tried to reason with her. Sometimes I would hide from her. Other times I would make her laugh and even buy her presents. I tried to find a medicine that would cure her. When all else failed, I fought with her. Nothing worked.

I began to keep track of when the "Alien" would arrive each month. This technique seemed to help a little, but not quite enough. Everything negative was exaggerated during this time and if I was ready for the attack. . . if I could convince her that it was her hormones this time and not me . . . , if . . . , if only she were more like a man.

Now I am glad that I did not get my wish. What I was viewing as negative energy was actually the power source that keeps the human race on the planet. It is also the energy, although I did not know it at the time, that has always been the chief energy source for our pleasure.

We will call this type of energy "Tumescence" (Tu-mess-ence.) I think it will clear up a great many mysteries for you, as it did for me, about both men and women. Learning how to recognize tumescence and deal with it appropriately is one of the secrets to having more fun and happiness both in and out of bed.

One of the definitions in the dictionary explains tumescence as "being swollen, as with sexual energy. Sexual tension that is not being released or used."

For our purpose,I have expanded this definition to create some new distinctions that will help you to produce more pleasure in your life. I will use the word to describe a condition and a certain behavior that humans, especially females, occasionally exhibit.

The expanded definition of tumescence includes, among other things, the experience of being in heat. This can mean either an agitated or a pleasant feeling of being sexually aroused. Tumesced* (pronounced tu-messed) can also mean a particular type of tension, similar to a rubber band that is being twisted tighter and tighter. Tumescent energy can feel from anything like a warm glow, one time, to a raging fire the next. When tumescent energy is not out of control, it can produce pleasant feelings and inspire men to high levels of production.

*(From this point on, I will use this spelling and pronunciation, for ease of reference. A more accurate spelling might be "tumefied" or "tumid", but those spellings sound too much like something you would do to an Egyptian mummy and have proven awkward when I have tried to use them.)

Tumescence has many forms. Tumescent (tu-messent) energy is most commonly identified in the form of bitchiness or tension, as if the person were agitated by something or someone and all negative feelings are being magnified. At other times, however, when the tumescent energy is at a lower level and under control, the person feels pleasantly aroused and positive feelings are intensified.

WHERE DOES IT COME FROM?

First, it is necessary to understand that women have one heat cycle a month with two highs and also seasonal heat cycles that show up twice a year. The monthly heat cycle highs come around the time of ovulation and menstruation. The seasonal heat cycles come in the spring with a lesser cycle in the fall.

Somewhere around five days before a woman's period, her heat level or tumescent energy starts building up. She begins to get more and more tumescent as she gets closer to her period. During her period, this tumescence begins to subside until the time around ovulation when it starts to increase again. Another tidal wave of energy begins to build up power.

Historically, women have been mistreated when it comes to their heat cycles. There are times they probably would like to deny they even have them.

Most of us know that women are usually the most tumesced close to the time of their periods. Stories have been made up about this, such as the one which says that if the shadow of a woman on her period falls on a snake, the snake will crawl away and die.

The Indians were said to have built a special tent

and made their women stay in it during their periods.

No wonder women feel discriminated against and don't want to acknowledge their heat cycles.

For years some doctors refused to believe that there was any such thing as PMS. Some physicians called it an illness, gave drugs to try to "cure" it, and even operated to get rid of the symptoms. Most of the treatment was designed to try to flatten the woman's highs and lows. To make her more stable. To try to make her more like a man.

But, in general, men are duller than women. Men are basically slower thinking, more rigid, and less flexible. Worst of all, men are bound by logic. Women, on the other hand, are in general dynamic, impulsive, and exciting. To try to make women more like men would be a great waste of sexual energy. Instead of trying to eliminate the dynamic energy that women have, why not learn how to use it to increase the pleasure, productivity, and joy in our lives and relationships?

That is one of the purposes of this book. The main purpose of *THE ONE HOUR ORGASM* is entertainment. Entertainment in the form of having more pleasure and fun in your life both in and out of bed.

HOW DO YOU SPOT IT?

What are the signs of tumescence? Of course,

meanness is the major single sign, but there are many other signals that are useful if you become familiar with them.

Tumescence is the easiest to recognize in the form of anger, agitation, irritability, or being lustful, passionate, or highly sensitive. A tumesced person can also exhibit signs of clumsiness, lack of concentration, and disorientation.

The higher the level of tumescence and the longer it is sustained, the more radical the behavior usually becomes.

THE FIVE LEVELS OF TUMESCENCE

We will talk about Tumescence from this point on as a form of energy that is generated and transmitted by women. Tumescence takes on different characteristics and intensifies feelings depending upon the amount of tumescent energy that is present.

In *DIETS DON'T WORK*, when teaching people how to lose weight, we discuss the different levels of hunger which are felt by naturally thin people. The level five is called "not hungry." Level four is when you are a little bit hungry, three is called nice and hungry, two is when you begin to get irritable and cranky, and one is when you are STARVING!...you are going to eat NOW, and nobody had better be between you and the food.

Learning to recognize and anticipate levels of hunger and deal with them appropriately is one of the ways I teach overweight people how to lose weight without dieting. With *THE ONE HOUR ORGASM*, we can create a similar scale by reversing the numbers. We can then use these new distinctions to begin to recognize and deal with tumescent energy.

Level one could be called "flat" or all tumescent energy has been discharged. You feel mellow and totally relaxed.

Level two is when you are "a little turned on". . . things are starting to get interesting, you are looking forward with anticipation.

Level three is when you are feeling a glow, turned-on, pleasantly excited.

Level four is when you could start to get anxious, highly passionate, hot and bothered, on edge, irritable, or cranky. Tumescent energy begins to magnify feelings at this level whether they are positive or negative. For example, the hottest sex is available to you at this level and, on the other hand, most of your biggest fights happen at level four.

Level five is when you have let tumescence build up too high. You feel out of control, desperate, frantic, hostile, hypercritical, or bad tempered. You may notice that you scream and snarl a lot at this level. You do not look or feel attractive and usually act repulsively.

If your partner is at a level one and you want to play, you are going to need to raise their level of tumescence. If your mate is at a level five, you are going to have to bring them down a little bit before you will be able to get close enough to even touch them.

Tumescence can feel either comfortable and pleasurable or uncomfortable and even painful. Tumescence usually feels enjoyable if the tumescent energy is at a controllable level or if there are good prospects for releasing it. Tumescence can make you feel terrible if your tumescent energy has been at a high level for a long time and no hope for relief is in sight.

When you have control of your tumescence, it can make you feel turned on, glowing, pleasantly vulnerable, and emotionally mushy.

If you begin to consider the existence of tumescent energy, you will begin to notice that the behaviors of people change according to the amount of tumescent energy that is present. A person's behavior will also be affected by whether or not they think there is hope for the early release of the energy. If a person thinks that the built up tumescent energy is going to stay the same, without any relief, they will usually have a tendency to behave somewhat irrationally.

Tumescence also has the characteristic of being the kind of energy which you can pick up from someone else, and, if you know how, you can increase or decrease this tumescent energy in yourself or others at will.

Women who work or live together for a while usually begin to have the highs of their cycles at the same time. If this tumescent energy builds up too high and is not acknowledged and discharged in a pleasurable or consciously directed way, it begins to cause problems for the person who is feeling it and almost everyone else around her. The person feeling it sometimes feels cranky, righteous, irritated, on-edge, highly sensitive, and is many times illogical and unreasonable. She thrashes around feeling very uncomfortable and trying not to feel the feelings she is having. She looks all around, trying to figure out what is causing these feelings.

If her man is anywhere in the vicinity, guess who the easiest target to blame is?

Ten years ago, after discovering the principles that my book *DIETS DON'T WORK* was based on, I lost weight and by doing what naturally thin people do, have kept it off without dieting. One of the things that naturally thin people do is that they "forget" to eat sometimes. When I was overweight, I thought such forgetfulness was some form of brain damage, but now I notice that it is a fairly normal occurrence.

Now, when I start getting irritable, grouchy, unreasonable, and short-tempered, I check to see when I last ate. If it has been a long time, it is not hard to figure out that the people or circumstances around me are not the problem as much as the uncomfortable feelings of hunger that are being brought on because I haven't eaten.

Once I am aware that it is my hunger that is affecting me, I calm down and am more in control. If I am not hungry, I look around for the source of my tumescence.

As men, however, no matter how tumesced we get, we are told that we cannot under any circumstances experience tumescence in the same way that a woman does. As a man, can you remember a time when you felt that you were on YOUR period?

As a man, just imagine being four times more tumesced than you have ever felt. What if you had been that way for three days, nonstop, with no relief, and none in sight? What might your outlook on life be, and is it possible that you might be looking around for someone to blame or take it out on?

What I have just described is a condition many women report experiencing frequently. What if a man felt restless, edgy, ugly, bloated, unloved, misunderstood, ignored, and agitated a couple of times a month? Is it possible he might become a little unreasonable? Would he possibly allow himself to be pampered a little by getting his hair or nails done? Do you think it might be illogical if he went shopping and even bought something because it made him feel better?

Who do you find in the shopping malls most of the time? Women that have heat cycles or men? Who fills up aerobic classes to work off their excess energy? Who moves all the furniture around every spring? Who begs you to "talk" to them, give them attention, and spend time with them?

For now, all I want is to begin to introduce to you the behavior and feelings which I will describe by using the word tumescence. Notice how tumescence affects people and who is causing it.

I know this concept of tumescence is strange at first, but I want you to go along with the notion for a few days and begin to look at your life using this idea of the existence of tumescent energy. The main idea that I am suggesting is that maximum pleasure and one hour orgasms would not be possible unless you learn to deal with this particular energy.

At this time, most men have no idea how to deal with this type of female energy. Not knowing what to do with tumescent energy was only one of the ways I came to find that, like other men, I was dumb when it came to women.

WHAT ABOUT MEN?

Men do not have heat cycles. BUT, MEN USUAL-
LY GO INTO HEAT WHEN THEY ARE AROUND
WOMEN WHO ARE IN HEAT. Men who exercise
obsessively often do so to get rid of tumescence.
They may be around a lot of women who are
tumesced and have picked up their transmitted sexual energy.

If you have ever been around an older male dog,
you will see an example of a male mammal picking
up the signals from a female. The dog lays around,
sleeps a lot, and looks very bored. A female dog in
heat comes into the picture and suddenly you have
an alert, excited, and happy dog on your hands.

Men are able to pick up and respond to a woman's heat cycle signals, but only a woman has both
broadcasting and receiving equipment. IF A MAN IS
THINKING ABOUT SEX, IT IS BECAUSE HE HAS
RECEIVED A TRANSMITTED FEELING THAT
STARTED IN A WOMAN.* It doesn't make any
difference whether the woman is 19 or 89, whether she has had a hysterectomy or not, nor does it
make any difference if she is fat or thin. She may
not even be interested in doing anything with his
turned on state of mind and body. Maybe she just
likes to test out her equipment every once in a while.
*(A Men also has the ability to become tumesced by
imagining that a woman desires him or is available

to him as a sexual partner such as when he is reading Playboy magazine.)

There is a story about the male Panda bear which
demonstrates the theory I am proposing. The male
Panda spends the whole year up in some bamboo
tree, calmly munching on bamboo leaves. Once
every year or even longer, the female Panda goes
into heat. According to the story, she can be five to
ten miles away, and yet the male Panda senses her
change of condition and begins to run through the
forest until he finds her. They mate and then the
male Panda returns to his bamboo tree to once again
munch leaves.

Of course, humans are not bears or dogs, but, I
want you to consider this possibility that females are
the source of male sexual excitement. Unless a man
has been around a woman who is sexually aroused,
he will not be turned on. This is contrary to what
most of us have been brought up to believe. It goes
against the notion that men are the sexual aggres-
sors and women put up with men's sexual appetites.

I am proposing that men get the blame for sex,
but are actually the romantics, and that women get
the blame for romance, but are the source of sexual
arousal. Men are walking around wanting to find
someone to be romantic with, but pretending that
they are not romantic. Women are pretending that
they are romantic, but are actually the source of sexual excitement.

If you accept the concept that women are the source of sexual arousal, you will find many benefits that come along with this idea. One, is that if you are a man, you never have to worry about being turned on. Whenever the woman in your life wants you, she will let you know in a way you can't ignore. (Actually, you can ignore it, but she will cause you pain if you do.) Another benefit is that if you are a woman, this concept puts you in the driver's seat. Couples, who have worked with the idea that women are in charge, have been pleased with the positive results in their sex life and relationship. For now, just keep an open mind.

HOW TO BEST USE THIS BOOK

It is important to keep a diary while you are reading and applying the information you are about to receive. This book is set up to help you keep your "diary" notes for handy reference.

You will probably resist keeping a diary and everything else the book asks you to do. Why? Dr. Baranco says it is because, in our culture, we are not able to tolerate very much pleasure. If you are like me, you will not believe Dr. Baranco's premise and will have a lot of arguments. That's fine! When you come up with reasons why you resist following the instructions in the book, just pretend that 90% of your reasons come about because you can't stand the amount of pleasure that you are being promised and do them anyway.

THE ONE HOUR ORGASM is a recipe and formula for pleasure and relationships beyond your wildest dreams. It is a long recipe, but a very exact one. You have the choice to follow it exactly and see for yourself if the promises of the book are true or not. Or, you can add your own ingredients and leave out other parts and then blame the recipe for the limited results you receive.

I have spent a lot of time and care making sure all of the steps are in order and recommend that you do not skip around or stop too long between one step and the next. Nothing in this book is intended to do anything other than make you and your relationship better than it is now.

Chapter 2

MEN VS. WOMEN

WHY WOMEN ARE MEAN
(ESPECIALLY TO THEIR MEN)

In western culture, women have always been treated like second class citizens and have been discriminated against in many areas. For one thing, women report that they have had fewer orgasms than men. Men get to have orgasms almost every time they have intercourse, but women usually don't.

A woman may think she has earned the right to be angry with the man in her life. Every man who has not given her what she wanted has made her

---

even more angry. One of the ways she has to release her anger is to take it out on her present man.

So, if most women would really like to have better sex lives, why don't they?

MEN ARE DUMB
WHEN IT COMES TO WOMEN

I really did expect the women in my life to be like me, a man. We are both human, aren't we? We both have intellect and reason and passion.

Yes, but only women have heat cycles, which may be the thing that makes most of them smarter, more dynamic, and more intuitive.

As men, one of our problems is that women expect too much of us. We don't know what to do to make them happy or even how to talk to them. When growing up, most men are taught not to show fear or weakness and yet, on the other hand, women are taught that it is O.K. to express their feelings.

Another problem is that we, as men, have very seldom been told the truth about our performance with women . . . until we marry one of them. Men that are the most handsome, rich, or popular suffer the most from being lied to about how well they perform.

Handsome, rich, and popular men are the most sought after by women. A smart woman does not want to run a man off by stepping on his ego, and the area that is the most important and sensitive to a man is his performance, especially in bed.

There is only one answer to having a really successful relationship with a man. You, as women, need to be willing to train us and tell us the truth. On our part, we men have to admit how dumb we are, how little we have been trained, and that we are trainable.

Training us, telling us the truth, and getting us to say that we are willing to be trained is easier said than done. It seems that we, as men, will never give up trying to prove that we are not dumb when it comes to women.

One of the problems that a man secretly fears is his inability to satisfy and please his woman. When most women hear that one hour orgasms are possible, they are elated. But, when men hear this news, their anxiety levels go way up. It has been hard enough to get a woman to say that she has had an orgasm. Now we are going to be expected to keep it going for an hour!

Relax. Just follow the instructions I'm going to give you, and you will be able to perform better, under any circumstances, than you have ever dreamed possible.

The only question is: Are you going to be smart enough to follow some simple instructions without leaving any out or trying to add any of your own? Please don't do what I did. Don't attempt to look smart by trying to prove you're not dumb.

Chapter 3

HOW TO GET INTO BED WITH CONFIDENCE

———————————•———————————

How would you go about playing tennis or golf with confidence? What would you do before you showed up at Wimbledon to play in the tennis championships? "Practice!" you probably would say.

Of course. And yet we are not "supposed" to have sex before marriage or even talk about it. However, on our wedding night, we are to jump into bed and perform perfectly.

What if you were not allowed to play tennis, practice it, talk about it, or even use the language of tennis? Imagine that you were even too embarrassed to ask someone else. What if everyone else pretended

———————————•———————————

that they already knew everything there was to know about tennis and would make fun of you if you asked? Then one day you got married and the next day you were to show up at Wimbledon and win!

Ridiculous? Who did you learn about sex from? One of your friends? How old were they? Seven years old? Twelve years old? Do you remember your first conversation about sex? Who was the conversation with and what did you learn?

_____

_____

_____

_____

Have you ever thought about where the people got their information whom you learned about sex from? Maybe an "older" brother or sister. How old? Thirteen? Fifteen?

If a sex course were offered by a 15-year-old child, would you go?

If you have been good by our society's standards, how good do you think your sex life is going to be?

Is it any wonder that "good" people find themselves going outside their marriages and causing tremendous problems? If you got everything possible out of an exceptional sex life with your partner, what need would there be to go outside your marriage?

If a man goes outside the marriage for more sex, how does his wife interpret that action? In addition to feeling hurt and betrayed, most likely she would feel guilty in some way. Maybe, if she was adequate, her mate would not have needed anyone else. His wife may even begin to think it is because she is getting older, fatter, less beautiful, or too demanding. Something about her must not be good enough.

The main reason that people go outside their marriages is because they stop feeling like they are winning with each other. They are no longer having enough fun. All they hear are complaints, problems, and dissatisfactions. They begin to realize they aren't pleasing each other, and the solution begins to look like finding someone they can win with.

According to a recent survey reported by Dr. Joyce Brothers in her syndicated column, satisfactory sex relations have been taking the average couple about six years to work out, although 12 percent say they made a satisfactory adjustment within the first year. Often husbands thought that sexual adjustment had been made, but the wives disagreed.

If you, as women, want the best sex possible, you'll have to start telling us the truth in a way that makes us want to give you what you want. You do not have to figure out how to do this on your own. It has already been worked out for you. Just follow the instructions that will follow, step by step.

Chapter 4

WHAT HOLDS US BACK?

———————————•———————————

The first exercise may not look important, but the "recipe" for pleasure and getting more out of your relationship is very exact. If you skip around or leave out some of the steps, you are most likely going to wind up with what you already have.

Without "thinking" too much, WRITE OUT all the "Don'ts" you can remember about the subjects listed below. Do not hold anything back. Write down everything that pops into your mind, no matter how silly it may seem. It is very important that you WRITE down your answers, not merely think of them.

———————————•———————————

Even before we learn to speak, we begin to accumulate behaviors which we discover are and are not acceptable to others. After a while, our list of DO'S and DON'TS become an automatic part of us. After you complete your list, I will ask you to go back and examine which ones keep you from experiencing as much pleasure as is possible.

Let yourself have some fun doing this exercise. If you have to, guess at or make up what your "Don'ts" might be.

WHAT ARE YOUR "DON'TS" REGARDING:

Your body: (Example: Don't have bad body odor)

_____

_____

_____

_____

_____

_____

Other people's bodies: (Example: Don't stare at them) _____

_____

_____

_____

_____

_____

What you feel: (Example: Don't cry)_____

_____

_____

_____

_____

_____

_____

What others feel: (Example: Don't make anyone
angry)_____

_____

_____

_____

_____

_____

_____

Your sex organs: (Example: Don't touch them in
public) _____

_____

_____

_____

_____

_____

The opposite sex's sex organs: (Example: Don't acknowledge they have any) _____

_____

_____

_____

_____

_____

Your sex practices: (Example: Don't talk about them)

_____

_____

_____

_____

_____

_____

Your partner's sexual performance: (Example: Don't tell your partner the truth if it is negative) _____

_____

_____

_____

_____

_____

Eating: (Example: Don't leave anything on your plate) _____

_____

_____

_____

_____

_____

Sleeping: (Example: Don't snore) _____

_____

_____

_____

_____

_____

OTHER DON'TS: _____

_____

_____

_____

_____

_____

_____

_____

_____

_____

_____

(Add paper if you need more room)

As we go along, you will discover more of your "DON'TS" and you may come back and add them to your list.

Chapter 5

THE ANSWER

The major complaint sex therapists hear today is that their patients "want to make love" but they "don't want to."

Many times a woman will ask why the spark has left her marriage. Her husband does not want to make love to her as much as when they were first married. Usually the man is not involved with anyone else, and it is hard to understand why, after only a short number of years, he is so disinterested.

THE ONE HOUR ORGASM method will help solve this problem should it ever occur for you or your mate. You can pleasure your partner or be pleasured

---

with almost no concern about the mood or frame of mind either of you are in at the moment. This method puts the total control to pleasure or be pleasured in your hands. You never again have to wait around until the mood strikes, the moon is full, or whatever sign you were looking for to tell you that the time is right.

You will want to "do it" because you will know that every moment is going to be pleasurable.

Write down what you would like to get out of reading this book and doing all the exercises. Write down sexual and personal goals. If you could have every part of your life exactly the way you wanted it, what would each part of your life be like? Be specific.

_____

_____

_____

_____

_____

_____

_____

_____

_____

_____

_____

_____

_____

_____

_____

(Add paper if you need more room)

It will be interesting to go back over this list when you have finished the book.

You are on your way to discovering what may be holding you back from being the best you can be in your sex life. Your relationship is going to be even better than it is now.

BEGINNING YOUR
ONE HOUR ORGASMS

You have been waiting to find out how to achieve a one hour orgasm. You really want to know, and you want to begin to feel the pleasure that you can imagine will be there for you and your mate, right?

Not necessarily. You will probably start to come up with a lot of other things to do and reasons not to follow the "Recipe" I am about to give you. It is perfectly normal for you to doubt and think those thoughts. If you have a tendency to act in the way I just described, it is an excellent opportunity to notice how you tend to unconsciously resist pleasure.

It is natural that everything you can imagine will come up to prevent you from following these instructions, such as emergencies, need for food or a nap, laziness, boredom, "I don't want to, I'm tired, I haven't got the time, I just had a fight with my husband," etc..

Almost everyone who reads this book will feel that he or she is at least one level above everyone else who is reading the book and that it is not necessary to follow these instructions. Some of you will begin to feel very hostile, and it will sound like I am some teacher that you once had in school.

Don't worry. Just know that what you are feeling is resistance and go ahead and follow the instructions. Say "Thank you" to whatever thought or consideration you are having and do the next exercise anyway.

Describe all the excuses, "dreads," and resistance which tempt you not to complete this chapter:

_____

_____

_____

_____

_____

_____

_____

Would you consider enjoying your resistance and go on anyway? Just lighten up. If you feel like you are in the molasses of procrastination, you do not have to fight it. Just go into slow motion. Slowly do one sentence at a time. Get a sense that you are winning by moving forward, but don't stop. Slow down until the feeling of resistance passes.

SHOPPING LIST

The first things you need are the following

supplies and equipment. Round them up or go shopping for them right away.

1.   A large hand mirror. Not a compact mirror. It must be at least as large as your outstretched hand.

2.   A full-length mirror. You can go to a discount store and buy a five-foot mirror if you do not already have one. Lean it against your bedroom wall.

3.   A jar or tube of Vaseline. Get the brand "Vaseline" for this experience. You may eventually switch to another brand, but it is important that you start with Vaseline.

4.   Something to please your eyes such as candles, flowers, or a beautiful painting.

5.   Something to please your nose: scented bath oil, your favorite perfume or cologne, flowers, or scented candles.

6.   Something to please your ears: romantic music . . . a tape player with or without earphones, a blank cassette tape (optional), and a cassette tape of romantic music or radio tuned to a romantic station.

7.   Something to give pleasure to your taste buds . . . something wonderful to eat or drink. One of your simple favorite foods or drinks, such as a piece of chocolate or glass of freshly squeezed orange juice.

8. A private space where you can have all of the above assembled for at least 1½ hours without interruption. Also have access to a bathtub or shower. You may wish to borrow a friend's place or even to rent a hotel room.

9. A flashlight.

10. This book and a pen.

GET READY

There are five parts to this recipe. Complete one before you go on to the other. You will only know how important it is to do all parts of this exercise after you have completed all the steps. Until you are finished, just know that doing this exercise will make all the difference in the world to your future sex life.

The two most important ingredients are: your willingness to do the exercise to the best of your ability, and DOING IT.

1. How willing are you to do the exercise, right now?

_____

_____

_____

_____

_____●_____

_____

_____

If not, why? Write out your answers so you can
let go of your reservations.

_____

_____

_____

_____

_____

_____

_____

2.   Can you be counted on to do the exercise

      100%? _____

When? What day? What time?_____

_____

_____

_____●_____

Do you have any other considerations? If so, write them out so that you can let go of them or get them out of the way.

_____

_____

_____

_____

_____

_____

_____

Thank you for answering these questions. You are about to take the single biggest step you have ever taken in order to train your nervous system to have one hour orgasms.

You may be exercising aerobically to stay in shape and to keep your circulatory system healthy. You may even work out with weights to keep your body hard and fit. Why not work out your nervous system so that it can work better for you? If you do this regularly, you will be able to do things that you could not do otherwise.

WARNING. READING ABOUT THESE EXERCISES WILL DO YOU AS MUCH GOOD AS SENDING SOMEONE TO A GYM TO WORK OUT FOR YOU. If you don't do the exercises, you won't get the promised results. Do the following exercises.

Chapter 6

READY? GET SET? GO!!

The first step you are asked to undertake takes thirty minutes after you read through all of the instructions. You could spend hours just to complete the next step, but do not spend any more time on it than thirty minutes. Taking too much time is a sign of resisting.

Dr. Baranco calls this the "Visiting Dignitary" part of the exercise. He suggests that you pretend that a very important person has requested to use a room in your home. Imagine that it is someone very special. Maybe a movie star, a world leader, or visiting royalty such as Prince Charles or Princess Diana.

What do you do? Make the room as pleasurable as you can, given your time and resources, so that the time the dignitary spends there will be as memorable as possible. Don't hold back or compromise.

Have wonderful things around that will please each of the dignitary's senses. Make sure there are as many visually attractive items to look at as you can arrange. Throw any clutter in a closet or out of sight. Set out your candles next to your matches so you can light them when you are ready. Set the flowers out where they can be visually enjoyed from anywhere in the room.

Have music set up and playing softly so that the dignitary's ears will experience pleasure.

Have some perfume or cologne available so your guest can dash some lightly on his or her body. Some scented candles might be a nice touch.

Have something ready that will please your guest's taste buds.

Make sure the bathroom is clean. It would be nice to offer a bubble bath or shower, using the best soap and fragrances you have.

REMEMBER: STOP GETTING READY AS SOON AS YOUR THIRTY MINUTES ARE UP.

CHANGE IN PLANS

After everything has been set up, imagine that the phone rings and your movie star, world leader, or royalty has had to cancel. O.K. . . . No use letting all these preparations go to waste, is there?

You can use this wonderful space you have set up to accomplish some great things for yourself. Ready?

SENSUAL BATH (15 Minutes)

The purpose of taking a bath is to begin to please yourself and open your body up to feelings of pleasure.

Go to the bathroom and set out your candles and sweet fragrances such as perfume, cologne, bubble bath, and bath oils. Draw your bath with just the temperature and fragrance you want. Undress, hanging or folding your clothes nicely and neatly. Slowly and sensually let yourself down into the bath water. Savor how the water feels as it touches each part of your body. Splash the water on different parts to see how good the water feels to your skin. What parts of you are enjoying the bath the most? Can you do something to allow the other parts of your body to also enjoy the feel of the water? How much can you let yourself experience the light from the candles and the sweet fragrances?

After you get out of the bath, slowly and gently dry yourself off. Jot down anything that you found pleasurable and want to remember about the experience you just had.

_____

_____

_____

_____

_____

If you gave your mate a sensual bath, how much pleasure would they get out of the experience and how much would they appreciate it?

_____

_____

_____

_____

BODY INVENTORY (15 Minutes)

This next part of the exercise is very important. Do not leave any part of your body out.

Like most humans, you probably are not very proud of parts of your body...parts you actually may have no reason not to be proud of. Many people cannot quickly think of even one thing they like about their bodies. Why do you suppose that is? There must be some value in beating yourself up or else why do so many of us do it?

Do you remember, when you were a child, your parents punishing you in some way? They either used physical punishment or verbal scolding or both. Did you ever wonder why they punished you?

The purpose of punishment is to make you behave in a better way. In other words, make you better. You may have noticed, that, in your case, it did not work. You probably didn't get better...you just got sneaky and covert. And if you were smart, you no longer did whatever they had punished you for. At least, not in front of them.

One day you grew up. You wanted to get better and your parents were not around. What did you do? You learned how to beat yourself up, not physically, but in more subtle ways.

Have you ever deprived yourself of something,

like some new clothes, until you lose some more weight? Do you remember ever standing in front of a mirror saying derogatory things about yourself? "Look at those fat thighs! What an ugly body! Look at that flabby skin. I could just throw up! How could anyone who looks like that go out in public?

If you don't think that saying things like that to yourself is abusive, try this. Go to your favorite store and stand outside. As people come out, say the same things to them as you do to yourself. "Look at those fat thighs!" and so on. It won't take you long to recognize how abusive you have been to yourself.

Beating yourself up doesn't work. You don't get better. It is like going out to your garden every day and only watering the weeds. Anything that you give attention to expands. Why give attention to the negative things. Either do something to fix them or learn to love them.

Dr. Baranco says that you should do the next part of the exercise alone. The first time my wife and I did this exercise, we both "forgot" to do a lot of the things we were instructed to do. We went blank. During our second effort, we did the parts of the exercise that we had left out the first time and got an enormous amount more out of this exercise.

I felt that I would have done better the first time if I had asked my wife to assist me. So much resistance came up for me at this part of the exercise.

I felt tired! I didn't feel like doing it! I didn't think it was worth the effort. I would have experienced more pleasure doing the exercise if I had asked my wife for support. Of course, she would have had to be enthusiastic about helping me for it to work.

If you want to be helped through the exercise, but your partner is not completely willing, do it on your own first. I invite you to ask your spouse to be your coach the first or even the second time you do this Visual Inventory part of the exercise.

If either of you does not want to do the exercise together, another alternative is to use a tape recorder. First, record all of the instructions, step by step, that you will be asked to follow. Play them back to yourself as you are going through the exercises. It may be easier for you to turn the tape recorder on and off, instead of going back and forth to the book.

Are you ready? Make sure the place you are using is warm enough for you to be nude for about one hour.

VISUAL INVENTORY

1. With all your clothes off, get the hand mirror and go over to your full length mirror. Your job is to find every area of your body about which you can FIND SOMETHING TO LIKE. I know how very easy it is for you to find things you do not like

about your body. WHEN YOU LOOK INTO THE MIRROR, YOU ARE USUALLY LOOKING FOR WHAT IS WRONG WITH YOU. Your attention tends only to be on the bad parts. You keep saying and demonstrating that you are disappointed in your body. You keep watering the weeds.

Now it is time to cross the line over to being a person committed to pleasure; look only and specifically for things you like about your body. If you come across an area you can find absolutely nothing good about, even if you bend over backwards, pass by it quickly and let go of that judgment. Go on to the next area.

2. Start with the top of your head or, if your mate is coaching you, have her start there at the top and guide you to any areas you may leave out. See what you look like from a bird's point of view. Say out loud the good and interesting things that you see. You will need both mirrors to do this properly. See what different shades of colors you can notice and what different shapes you can make out as you explore each area.

When you look at your ears, wiggle them around with your fingers. Do the same as you come to any part of your body that is a working or movable part. See how it looks and feels to move it around.

Notice the direction in which your hair grows. Lightly touch your body hair and notice that, like a cat's whiskers, you can pick up sensory input by touching it. Also lightly and lovingly touch the hair on your eyebrows and eyelids.

Examine your whole head. Look closely at the skin. Notice the different colors and types of skin in each area. See if both eyes are exactly the same. Look at your lips and open them to see if the skin inside of your mouth is like the skin on your lips.

Jot down the things you like or could learn to like about parts of your head and facial features (or have your partner write out the answers for you as you go along. Have the answers read back to you at the end of each segment to make sure there is nothing you have left out.)

_____

_____

_____

_____

_____

_____

_____

_____

_____

_____

_____

(Add paper if you need more room)

3. Next, stand over and straddle your hand held mirror and see what you look like to the shower drain. Then get your flashlight and squat over your mirror and see what your rectum looks like. Have you looked at your rectum in the last year? You probably think you do not want to know what it looks like. Most people imagine that it is going to look horrible and disgusting. Look anyway and see if you can find anything attractive about it. Also, be sure to thoroughly examine your sexual organs before moving on to examine other areas.

If you are a woman, can you see how the outside of your vagina looks somewhat like a flower? Do you see the petals?

As you look at the different parts of your body, see if you can begin to notice the different colors and types of skin tissue.

Do you need to be as embarrassed or ashamed as you are about your body parts?

_____

_____

_____

_____

_____

_____

Jot down all the things you like or could learn to like about the parts of your groin area and why.

_____

_____

_____

_____

_____

4. Now, starting with the bottoms of your feet, look at every part of your body that you have not

examined yet.

Remember, you are looking for things to like. Be aware and interested in the different colors and kinds of skin in each area. Use both mirrors when necessary to see yourself from every angle. Don't forget your back.

As you go along, jot down all the things you like or could learn to like about these other parts.

_____

_____

_____

_____

_____

_____

_____

_____

_____

5. Using the full length mirror, try different poses and positions that make you look the most alluring. Try different angles.

Jot down all the angles and poses that you like or could learn to like.

_____

_____

_____

_____

_____

_____

_____

6. What parts of your body have you really never noticed before? What parts surprised you by their color or shape?

_____

_____

_____

_____

_____

_____

_____

_____

_____

You will discover the value of these exercises only after you have done all the exercises in sequence.

You may have already made one important observation. If you did this exercise properly, you looked for what you liked about your body.

A. How is looking for what is good about your body different than what you usually do? Do you usually look for what is wrong, beat yourself up, or blank out parts of your body?

_____

_____

_____

_____

_____

_____

_____

_____

B. What is the profit in always looking for what is wrong with your body? What do you suppose you get out of it?

_____

_____

_____

_____

_____

_____

C. What did you discover by looking for what is right about your body?

_____

_____

_____

_____

_____

_____

_____

_____

_____

· D. Do you think you will be able to begin to look for what you enjoy in your partner's body more after this exercise?

If so, why? _____

_____

_____

_____

_____

_____

E. Do you think you will be able to begin to look for what you enjoy in your own body more after this exercise, rather than automatically checking for what is wrong? Why?

_____

_____

_____

_____

_____

_____

F. Which do you get the most pleasure from:

_____ 1. Looking only for the bad when you look at your body or your partner's?

_____ 2. Looking only for the good when you look at your body or your partner's?

According to a recent study, only one out of every ten people will admit to being at their ideal weight. They don't like at least some part of their body. It is a miracle, isn't it, that very many of us have the nerve to take our clothes off and let another person see us? This kind of negative perception about our body, as Spock would say, "seems illogical."

TACTILE INVENTORY (15 Minutes)

On this part of the exercise you may want to start out by having your partner read all of the instructions to you or record them for you to play back to yourself. You will usually want to be left alone to complete this part of the exercise.

WHY "TURN ON" YOUR BODY?

If you were lying on your stomach and someone set a sixty pound weight on your buttocks, would you be aware of it? "Sure!", you say. Did you know there is sixty to one hundred pounds of weight on your backside right now if you are sitting? Are you aware of the pressure?

When you are wearing shoes, your feet are usually hurting. Why aren't you aware? Because you have learned to turn "off" parts of your body. To shut down, not feel, to blank out or non-confront feelings that you do not want to feel. The problem is that now we need to turn your body back on in order to receive and give maximum pleasure.

One of the main differences between pleasure and pain is the amount of pressure applied. Varying amounts of pressure can feel pleasurable sometimes and painful at other times.

One of the purposes of having you sensitize and become more aware of your body is to enable you to be able to tell your partner what feels good to you and have your partner be able to tell you what feels good to them.

Another reason for doing this exercise is to connect the areas of your body which are less sensitive with parts that are more sensitive. You will discover that a touch in one area can actually be pleasurably felt in another.

Your only job during this exercise is to feel pleasure and pressure. If you are having any thoughts or feelings of resistance or want to do this exercise later, write why you want to put it off.

_____

_____

_____

_____

_____

_____

_____

Thank your "mind" for sharing those thoughts with you and continue anyway. The more resistance you feel, the slower you should start out. Slowly take and understand one sentence at a time if you have to.

HOW DO YOU "FEEL?"

First, get out your jar of Vaseline and a large towel or sheet. Put the towel or sheet over the bed or place where you are going to sit or lie down.

Start by pinching the skin over your elbow as hard as you can. Do you notice how insensitive this area is? Not much feeling, is there?

Now pinch with equal pressure the skin on the inside of your elbow. Your sensing ability varies from one area to the other, doesn't it?

USE A "TAKING TOUCH"

When you touch velvet, does the velvet feel good or does your hand? Your hand does, of course. Touching velvet is an example of a "Taking Touch." Intend to "take" pleasure when you are touching yourself.

There is little need to be concerned about "giving" pleasure. If it feels good to your touch, it will almost always feel good to the person you are touching.

Notice that when you are aware of "taking" pleasure, you also feel the pleasure of being touched. You will begin to discover that what feels best to you will probably feel good to your partner.

Next, with your fingers, make circles on the inside of your forearm. Notice the speed and pressure that feels the best, both to your fingers and also to your skin.

Touch your skin with the edge and even the backs of your fingernails. Also, try touching yourself lovingly with just the hairs on your hand. Can you "take" pleasuring sensations with your nails? How does your skin like being touched this way?

Now, see what it feels like to use a little lubricant. Get a very small amount of Vaseline and warm it up by rubbing a small amount in your hands. Apply it to the inside of your forearm. Use small circular movements. Compare how different this feels versus rubbing "dry." Do you notice that using the lubricant causes the sensations to spread, like the ripples in a pond when a pebble hits the water?

Begin to explore both sides of your upper and lower arm; lightly touch the hair to see how that feels. Do the same to your hands and fingers, shoulders, neck, face, eyes, ears, and especially your upper lip. From time to time try using Vaseline on different areas.

Notice the difference between rubbing your lower and upper lips. Which lip is the most sensitive? Does the inside of your lip or the outside have more feeling? When you touch your lips, can you feel pleasant sensations in your genital area?

Move on to your chest, nipples, stomach, sides, all sides of your legs, the tops and bottoms of your feet, and your toes. Pay special attention to your middle toe. Many people report pleasant sexual feelings from rubbing it.

Last, begin to explore your genital area.

Men: At this point, skip past the "WOMEN ONLY" section to the part marked "MEN ONLY". Don't worry. You won't miss anything. Later, you will be instructed to come back and read this section.

WOMEN ONLY:

The crotch area will be the most sensitive area of your body. Start on the far outer edges of your crotch. Make big circles across the lower part of your stomach, down the top part of your thigh, and crossing over just underneath the groin, outside your pubic hair area, and then back up to your stomach.

Slowly make the circle smaller and smaller until you begin to feel the pubic hairs. Gently begin to stroke the hairs with your fingers and both sides of your hand. Remember to continue to use "taking" touches.

Next, feel the outer lips of your vagina. It is a good idea to begin to apply Vaseline to the area you are touching. Slowly work in toward the inner lips. Notice which places are the most sensitive. Rub the opening to your vagina and also the outside of the hole to the urethra, which is your urinary opening.

Feel inside the opening of your vagina. Make sure you have plenty of Vaseline on your fingers and with one or two fingers, reach as far inside the vaginal canal as you can. Press against the vaginal wall with increasing pressure. Start with very light pressure at first and then find out how much pressure you can apply without feeling any pain.

Push at 6 o'clock or toward the floor and then at 3 o'clock and 9 o'clock. Lastly, push against the upper part or 12 o'clock. When you press against this last position, you may be able to feel stimulation as if you were pushing against the back of your clitoris. This "G-Spot" area may feel uncomfortable to your touch except just prior to and during an orgasm.

Now, begin to explore your clitoris. Make sure you have plenty of warm lubricant on your fingers. Feel the hood that covers the clitoris. This piece of skin is like the foreskin on a man before he is circumcised.

** DO NOT CAUSE AN ORGASM WHILE YOU ARE DOING THIS EXERCISE. IF YOU BECOME TOO EXCITED . . . STOP OR SLOW DOWN UNTIL YOU REGAIN CONTROL.

Pull the hood back and rub on the clitoris as high as possible. Begin to explore all sides of it. For most women the upper left side is the most sensitive.

Lastly, begin to explore the area around your second most sensitive area, your anus. There are many nerve endings close to this area. Again, make sure you are using a lubricant while you are exploring this area.

You have completed this part of the exercise. Go wash the lubricant off your hands and get ready for the next part.

For now, skip past the next "MEN ONLY" section to the part for "MEN AND WOMEN".

MEN ONLY:

The crotch area will be the most sensitive area of your body. Start on the far outer edges of your crotch and make big circles across the lower part of your stomach, down the top part of your thigh, crossing over just underneath the groin area and then back up to your stomach.

Slowly make the circle smaller and smaller until

---

you begin to feel the pubic hairs. Gently begin to lightly stroke the hairs with your fingers.

Next, take a liberal amount of Vaseline and rub it between your hands to warm it. Begin to apply the Vaseline to your penis and scrotum, the sack that surrounds your testicles.

Begin to feel the different parts of your penis. Start with the urethra opening, the hole at the end of your penis. Next, work on the crown, which is the area around the hole, and work down to the ridge of the crown.

Notice where you have the most pleasurable sensations. See if there is more feeling on one side than the other or in one spot versus another.

** DO NOT CAUSE AN ORGASM WHILE YOU ARE DOING THIS EXERCISE. IF YOU BECOME TOO EXCITED . . . STOP OR SLOW DOWN UNTIL YOU REGAIN CONTROL.

Work down to the shaft of the penis. Notice that the sides and top of the shaft have less feeling than the bottom part. The upper part, toward the crown, may have more feeling than the lower part.

Grasp the base of the shaft of the penis by wrapping your thumb and forefinger around it and press down. Next, wrap the thumb and forefinger of your other hand around the top of the sack of your testicles. Now, slowly pull down with increasing pressure and see how much pressure your testicles can take.

Surprised? Wait until you try this next part. With your lower hand surround your testicles and begin to squeeze them in a downward motion. Increase the pressure slowly until you feel discomfort or until you can squeeze no harder, whichever comes first.

Lastly, put some more Vaseline on your fingers and lubricate the area around your anus. Explore this area with your fingers and notice the areas which are the most sensitive.

Press in, with increasing pressure, on the area between your anus and the sack of your scrotum. The prostate lies buried inside this area and it is sensitive to pleasurable sensations.

You have now completed this part of the exercise. Go wash the lubricant off your hands and get ready for the next part.

MASTURBATION FOR PLEASURABLE EFFECT FOR BOTH MEN AND WOMEN

YOU HAVE TO KNOW WHAT YOU WANT BEFORE YOU CAN TELL ANYONE ELSE WHAT YOU WANT

The goal of the exercise is to feel as good as possible for as long as possible. Orgasm is not the purpose of this exercise and should be avoided in order to get the most value.

Some of the sex many men have experienced in the past might possibly be compared to going to the symphony in time to hear the last note and then either leaving or falling asleep.

What if we ignored the other parts of the symphony? Making the reservations, planning what to wear, dressing, having dinner before, entering the auditorium, slipping into our seats, and feeling the excitement before the curtain opens? Even after the last note is played and the applause is over, what about talking about it and enjoying the way we feel afterwards?

THE ONE HOUR ORGASM is about learning to enjoy the whole symphony of sensual pleasure, from beginning to end.

BEGIN

Do this exercise by yourself. Read all of the instructions before you begin. Record them on your tape recorder if you wish to play them back to yourself as you are doing the exercise. Use Vaseline from time to time in this process. Make sure your towel is handy, light your candles, turn on your music, and have your favorite food or drink setting out.

Start by rubbing your body in sensitive places as far away from the genitals as possible. Go slow and take your time. Work, area by area, toward your genitals. When you get tired or bored with rubbing on one area, go on to the next.

Try out different kinds of pressure from heavy to very light. See which one you like the best. Also, try different speeds from fast to very slow.

If you know how to touch yourself, you will know how to tell your partner to touch you. You will also better understand what will feel the best when you touch your partner.

TEASING

Before you get to your genital area . . . tease a place on your body. You will do this by causing a feeling of scarcity in one place and creating an abundance of feeling in another. Try the area around your nipples, or your navel, or even the inside of your thigh. To tease an area, start on the outside of whatever area you are working on. Make large circles around the spot you are teasing and slowly move in toward the center using smaller and smaller circles.

When the place you are teasing begins to anticipate that you are about to rub it, tease it some more by rubbing a different spot. It is as if you are creating an "itch" that wants to be scratched. Begin to notice that you have the power to create some interesting effects when working on your body. Later, you will be able to cause the same sensations when you are working on your partner's body.

Notice how you feel when you are being agitated or tumesced. Then—when you are good and ready—touch the area you have been teasing.

What you have been doing is an exercise in tumescence: to begin to play with the sexual energy in your body, to increase and decrease tension at your command. Relax and enjoy the exercise. There is no pressure on you to perform sexually or accomplish a result. Pleasure is your only goal.

"PEAKING"

"Peaking" is a technique that is designed to increase your ability to feel. As you are rubbing yourself and begin to feel the sexual pressure or tumescence build up in you, stop rubbing or slow down, or change direction. Especially do this when you are on the verge of an orgasm. As tumescence builds, bring yourself as close to the upper side of that feeling as is possible without going over the top . . . then let yourself down by stopping, slowing down, changing to a lighter pressure, or changing the direction you are rubbing.

You will notice that each time you build up to the

edge, the intensity of the feeling increases. If you continue to do this, you will be able to build the intensity to the highest point possible.

On a graph, peaking would look like this:

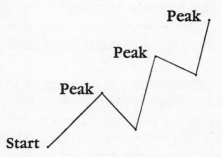

Notice that on the graph, the peaks keep going up to higher levels. Without "peaking" you could not get to those levels.

Always do "Peaking" as long as it is pleasurable to you. Remember, your job here is to feel as good as possible for as long as possible.

Men: For now, skip past the "WOMEN ONLY" section.

WOMEN ONLY

Now begin to work in slowly toward the clitoris. Notice what other areas are pleasurable to touch. How much pressure feels the best?

There is no hurry. Take your time. Get as much

pleasurable sensation out of each place as you can before going onto the next part of your body.

When you get to the clitoris, begin to experiment. Where on your clitoris feels the best when you touch or stroke it? What do different amounts of pressure feel like? You may notice that the more tumesced or excited you are, the more pressure you can pleasantly take. Be sure that you continue to apply Vaseline to the area you are rubbing.

If an orgasm starts to build up, back it off by stopping, slowing the speed or direction, or moving to another area. By doing this, you are "peaking" your climax. The more often you can do this, the higher you will find your climax to be.

Orgasm is the release of built-up sexual energy or tumescence. The more you put into the "peaking" of your orgasm, the more you will get out of it. Even your climax will be longer and stronger than any you have ever had before.

** REMEMBER...DO NOT CAUSE AN ORGASM WHILE YOU ARE DOING THIS EXERCISE. IF YOU BECOME TOO EXCITED...STOP UNTIL YOU REGAIN CONTROL.

Right now, you are going for the longest and most pleasurable effect, not an orgasm.

"CONNECTIONS"

At some point, apply Vaseline to another place on your body such as your breast. Begin to "tease" this part of your body by stroking the outside edge of the area using wide circles. Move slowly toward the nipple or center. Once you reach the center, the nipple should be very excited and turned on.

Rub on that area with similar pressure and movement as you are rubbing on your clitoris. Try to set up some kind of intercommunication between the two areas. Take your hand off one place and see if you can feel an echo in the other. Keep switching back and forth.

It is possible to "connect" any two areas of your body using this technique. You will have an idea of what I am talking about if you grew up in the days of "petting." "Petting" is sexual stimulation without direct contact with the sexual organs. You learned to feel pleasurable feelings in the genital area when being kissed on the lips, neck, or ears.

Once you get an area turned on and connected, see if you can bring yourself to the edge of an orgasm using only the secondary area.

Do this "connecting" exercise using as many parts of your body as is pleasurable for you. You might try the middle toe of your left or right foot, your upper lip, your ear lobe, the inside of your elbow or thigh, and also the arch of your foot. Continue to do this exercise as long as it feels good.

STOPPING

Continue to "peak" yourself until you notice that the pleasurable feelings you were having are starting to go down or even bottom out. At any time that you stop having good feelings from doing this . . . stop! Just say out loud to yourself, "THIS CONCLUDES THE EXERCISE."

If you go too far and cannot stop yourself from having an orgasm during the exercise, before you climax say out loud, "THIS CONCLUDES THE EXERCISE." Do the same if you decide you want to have an orgasm after the exercise.

WHEN YOU ARE COMPLETE WITH THE EXERCISE, TAKE A FEW MOMENTS TO LIE STILL AND BE AWARE HOW EACH PART OF YOUR BODY IS FEELING. WHAT IS THE LEVEL OF YOUR SEXUAL TENSION OR TUMESCENCE? LOW? TOTALLY FLAT? DESCRIBE WHAT YOU FEEL.

_____

_____

_____

_____

Women: For now, skip past the "MEN ONLY" section.

MEN ONLY

Now begin to work in slowly toward the penis. Notice what other areas are pleasurable to touch and what level of pressure feels the best on them. There is no hurry. Take your time. Get as much pleasurable sensation out of each place as you can before going onto the next part of your body.

When you get to the penis, begin to experiment on the part that feels the best to you. How do different amounts of pressure and different strokes feel to you? You may notice that the more sexually excited or tumesced you are, the more pressure you can pleasantly take. Be sure that you continue to apply Vaseline to the area you are rubbing.

If an orgasm begins to build up too high, back it off by stopping, slowing the speed, or moving to another area. By doing this you are "peaking" your climax. The more often you can do this, the more intense your climax will be.

Orgasm is the release of built-up sexual energy or tumescence. The more you put into the "peaking" of your orgasm, the more you will get out of it. Even the climax will be longer and stronger than any you have ever had before.

** REMEMBER...DO NOT CAUSE AN ORGASM WHILE YOU ARE DOING THIS EXERCISE. IF YOU BECOME TOO EXCITED...STOP UNTIL YOU REGAIN CONTROL.

Right now, you are going for the longest and most pleasurable effect.

"CONNECTIONS"

At some point, put Vaseline on another place on your body such as your chest. Men have the same amount of nerve endings in their chest area as women do. What feels pleasurable to them will probably feel the same to you.

Begin to "tease" by stroking the outside edge of whichever area you are working on, using wide circles. Move slowly toward the center. Once you reach the center, that area should be very turned on and ready to receive pleasurable touching.

Rub on that area with similar pressure as you are using on your penis. Try to set up some kind of intercommunication between the two areas. Take your hand off one place and see if you can feel an echo in the other. Keep switching back and forth.

It is possible to "connect" any two areas of your body using this technique. You will have an idea of what I am talking about if you grew up in the days of "petting." "Petting" is sexual stimulation without direct contact with the sexual organs. You learned to feel pleasurable feelings in your genital area when being kissed on the lips, neck, and ears.

Once you get an area turned on and connected, see if you can bring yourself to the edge of an orgasm using only the secondary area.

Do this "connecting" exercise using as many parts of your body as is pleasurable for you. You might try the middle toe of your left or right foot, your upper lip, your ear lobe, the inside of your thigh, and also the arch of your foot. Continue to do this exercise as long as it feels good.

STOPPING

Continue to "peak" yourself until you notice that the pleasurable feelings you were having are starting to go down or even bottom out. At any time that you stop having good feelings from doing this . . . stop! Just say out loud to yourself, "THIS CONCLUDES THE EXERCISE."

If you go too far and cannot stop yourself from having an orgasm during the exercise, before you climax say out loud, "THIS CONCLUDES THE EXERCISE." Do the same if you decide you want to have an orgasm after the exercise.

WHEN YOU ARE FINISHED WITH THE EXERCISE, TAKE A FEW MOMENTS TO LIE STILL AND BE AWARE HOW EACH PART OF YOUR BODY IS FEELING. WHAT IS THE LEVEL OF YOUR SEXUAL ENERGY OR TUMESCENCE? LOW? TOTALLY FLAT? DESCRIBE WHAT YOU FEEL.

_____

_____

_____

_____

_____

_____

_____

Chapter 7

HOW DID YOU DO?

———————————————•———————————————

The purpose of this last exercise was to impart some crucial information that must be experienced, not merely read. Write out the answers to these questions:

1. Are you more aware of which parts of your body give you the most pleasure? If so, which parts and what kind of touching do they like best?

———————————————————————————————

———————————————————————————————

———————————————————————————————

———————————————•———————————————

_____

_____

_____

_____

_____

_____

2. Do you think you are now more aware of which parts of your partner's body might give them the most pleasure, and if so, which parts and what kind of touching will they like best?

_____

_____

_____

_____

_____

_____

_____

Where will your partner like the same kind or similar touching as you did?

_____

_____

_____

_____

_____

_____

_____

3. Are you beginning to see how you can give the highest pleasurable effect to yourself and your partner? _____

What specifically did you learn that will help you in pleasuring your partner?

_____

_____

_____

_____

_____

_____

_____

_____

4. Can you begin to see that, someday with practice, you will be able to "wipe your partner out with pleasure?"

_____

_____

_____

What effect do you suppose this will have on your relationship with your partner?

_____

_____

_____

_____

_____

_____

_____

5. What more could you have done for yourself as the "Visiting Dignitary?" What thoughts or considerations stopped you from doing more?

_____

_____

_____

_____

_____

_____

6. Write down a date when you will repeat all of the above "Visiting Dignitary" exercises.

It is important to repeat these exercises every month or two for about a year, especially if you are interested in having more and longer orgasms. The exercises are also beneficial if you are single and want to get ready to have a relationship.

No matter what your situation is at the present time, by following these instructions you will experience more fun and spontaneity in your life, both in and out of bed.

You will probably resist repeating these exercises, not because you don't want the benefits promised, but because you will resist having too much pleasure in your life.

The solution is very simple. All you need to do is to just stop doing the behavior. Right now, go to your calendar or appointment book and schedule dates with yourself on specific days at certain times of the day when you will repeat these exercises.

First, write down the specific dates and times you will repeat these exercises over the next twelve months

_____

_____

_____

Next, go to your calendar or appointment book and mark the "date" with yourself there. Begin to look forward to that "date" as if it were with the most important person in the world.

Sometime in the future you may want to borrow your partner's eyes and do the preceding exercises using their help. If you think this kind of support would be valuable, make a date with your partner, and get your mate to put it on their calendar. If you start to slip back into your resisting patterns of behavior, your partner's support may get you back on track.

SHOW AND TELL

Make an appointment with your partner to talk about how the experience of "Visiting Dignitary" was for each of you from beginning to end. Go over each detail and be especially specific with each other on what sensitive areas you discovered.

Give each other all the information on how your body works. Press for details. You are preparing each other with this information. It is necessary in order to fulfill the promise of the title of the book.

One of the purposes of these exercises was to begin to increase the amount of pleasure you can tolerate at one stretch. Tell each other if large amounts of pleasure became uncomfortable while you were doing the "Visiting Dignitary" exercise.

If you became uncomfortable and stopped early, what were the specific thoughts or feelings that caused you to stop?

_____

_____

_____

_____

_____

_____

_____

_____

Do you feel your pleasure limit has increased or decreased by doing the exercises? If so, in what ways?

_____

_____

_____

_____

_____

How many times did you "peak" yourself? _____

Which feelings did you experience when you "peaked" yourself?

Relaxed? ____

Peaceful? ____

Anxious? ____

More tension? ____

Other? _____

_____

_____

_____

In what ways were you able to control, either upward or downward, the sexual energy or tumescence in your body?

_____

_____

_____

_____

_____

_____

_____

Are some of the "connections" you set up still working? Can you rub some specific, sensitized part of your body and feel the pleasurable sensations in your genital area?_____

If so, where?_____

_____

_____

_____

_____

Chapter 8

HOW TO "TRAIN" YOUR MAN

Make sure your man always feels he is winning with you.

It is no fun for anyone to do anything if they feel they are not winning. The way to have your man feel like he is winning with you is to MAKE SURE HE WINS.

I once read about how giant killer whales are trained to jump over a rope set ten feet above water level. The trainer does not go out into the ocean and look for whales who know how to leap such an obstacle. If they did, they would probably experience what many women experience when they look for the already "trained" man. There are NOT a lot of trained men out there and the ones that are trained are probably already taken.

The way whales are trained is the way you need to train your man, and everyone else in your life for that matter, to give you what you want.

The following is the technique that whale trainers use. The trainer starts out with the rope under water. Every time the whale swims over the top of the rope, the trainer gives him a fish. If he swims under the rope, he doesn't get a fish.

Once the whale catches on and is winning every time, the trainer raises the rope a little. The trainer continues to do this until the rope lies on the surface of the water. Now the whale has to jump over the rope to get the fish. Once he masters jumping over the rope and getting the fish, the trainer begins to raise it higher and higher out of the water until it is ten or so feet high.

If the trainer started out by putting the rope ten feet over the water and waited until the whale figured out that he had to jump over the rope to get the fish, most whales would starve to death. What if every time they didn't jump over the rope, the trainer verbally beat them up or got mad or ignored them? It wouldn't be very motivating or effective, would it?

Simple, isn't it? But how many times in the past have you waited until your man performed perfectly before you gave him the "fish"? And how many times have you beat him up verbally or gotten mad and given him no acknowledgment at all when he tried and at least came close? What would a little compassion cost you?

Remember, very few women have been trained to know how to train their men. Thus, men are not very smart when it comes to women, especially the woman who is their partner. Without treating him with any disrespect, keep your request simple. Break down whatever you want him to do into small steps. Steps he can do easily and which make him feel he is winning with you.

HOW TO MAKE SURE YOUR MAN ALWAYS FEELS THAT HE'S WINNING WITH YOU

Imagine you had a dog that you loved very much. Your dog is not very smart, intuitive, or perceptive about your needs, but he likes you and really wants to please you. Every time the paper boy throws the paper, it lands in the street and the dog chews it up. What do you do?

You could ignore him and not feed him. You could scream at him and criticize him, in which case he would probably either run away, become unresponsive and remain dumb, or become a mean dog. (Am I beginning to describe any of the men in your life?)

Let's say that you praised your dog for what he did that was right. He FOUND the paper, didn't he? You say, "That was good. You found the paper. Thank you!", and you continue to praise him and give him a big hug.

Think of this situation from your dog's point of view. He won! He did something to please you and got rewarded. He isn't smart, but his problem is to figure out how to please you so he can get rewarded again. Make it easy for him. . . . TELL HIM!

Remember, make your request easy. The next step is NOT to get him to bring the paper in the house and drop the paper at your feet without chewing it up.

Ask him if he thinks he could bring the paper up onto the curb and chew it up there? "Great," he thinks. "I can do THAT!", and he does.

What do you do? Praise him and give him a hug every time he does what you asked and repeat your request sweetly and with optimism every time he does not. Soon the paper will be chewed up enthusiastically on the curb.

Once he is winning at this, you could ask to see if he could chew the paper up in the yard, then on the porch, then in the house, and finally ask him not to chew the paper up at all. Congratulations! You now have a happy, trained dog that loves to please you and get praised by you for making you happy. Everyone will want him, but as long as he is winning with you, he will not want to go anywhere else.

There are countless ways to use this training technique with your man. The one that concerns us right away is to make sure he feels he is winning with you around the area of sexing better. No matter what he does, say, "That was great. Thank you. Do you know what I would like even better?"

He asks, "What?"

And you say, "Could you rub a little higher?" (harder, softer, lower, lighter, etc.)

He thinks to himself, "Sure! I can do that."

And you say, "That is even better. Thank you." And if you want more improvement, just keep giving him simple requests that move him closer and closer to exactly what you want, and at the same time praise and reward him each step of the way.

Do you know how great it makes him feel when you jump up and down and get excited about something he did for you? The basic premise here is that he really does like you and wants to please you. He just doesn't know how. He is not able to read your mind and you are going to have to tell him in a way that makes him want to do it. Make it easy and fun and above all, make sure he wins every time out.

A word of warning. He may make great improvement in the beginning and then begin to slow down when he starts getting near the top of his potential, or he may start out very resistant and as time goes by respond better and better. Either way, you need to be careful at any time he is moving slowly. If you get impatient and don't slow down to match his improvement, he may want to find someone that has lower standards than yours so he will feel like he is winning. Just be sure to apply large amounts of compassion and patience when he is moving slowly and make every tiny move forward a big deal.

Chapter 9

HOW TO TRAIN
YOUR WOMAN

If you are a man and have read the preceding section, I'm sure, you have already figured out that what is good for the goose is good for the gander. You may be dumb, but you're not stupid.

The training cycle that I have been describing can also be used by you to train your woman to make YOU happy. You can likewise use it to train almost everyone else in your life that you come into contact with to give you whatever you want.

If you use the training cycle to train your mate, it is important that you use the same compassion, patience, and optimism with her as you would like if you were being trained.

It is very easy to become disrespectful, angry, and impatient when you are training someone, but being righteous is not going to get you what you want. Negative responses on your part will make whoever you are training feel like they can't please you, no matter what they do.

PANDORA'S BOX

By the way, in regard to this whole *ONE HOUR ORGASM* concept... expect trouble! If you have been with your woman any period of time, you have probably done a lot of dumb things and hurt her many times without even knowing it. She is probably very resentful, but has not felt safe enough or permission to express her anger in a way that she can let go of it.

Even if she hasn't already started, she will probably want to punish you for a very long time for all your past transgressions. She may feel you deserve it for how dumb you've been. For example, how many times did you have an orgasm and she did not? How many times have you screamed at her and scared her? How often did she have to tiptoe around on eggshells and not be able to tell you the truth because she was afraid you might leave her? How

many times have you not given her what she wanted . . . when she wanted it . . . for as long as she wanted it? And worse than all of that, how many times
have you put watching television, reading your
newspaper, other people, or your work before her,
thereby letting her know that they are more important than she is?

She may have also been abused by other men in
her life and you are the only one around on whom
she can take out her anger and hurt. Not fair, is it?

Of course, you could make it up to her by giving
her all the one hour orgasms she can handle. Or
begin to give her whatever she wants, whenever she
wants it, for as long as she wants it. That always
works.

The main thing is to be patient. Every once in a
while you might ask her if she has punished and beat
you up enough yet? She will probably lie and say
"Yes," and then do it again. She feels she has earned
the right by putting up with you and all the other
dumb men in her life for so long.

There is another side to this issue. Women need
to remember that they have some responsibility
when it comes to their own hurt and anger. They
can usually find that they played a small part in causing whatever happened to them. At the very least,
they can be responsible for how long they have been
carrying the hurt and anger around. Just because they

have a man that loves them is no reason not to be responsible for their own bitchiness, meanness, demands, erratic behavior, and past hurts or anger.

It is great to have a man who wants you to be happy all of the time. But you don't have the right to beat him up every time you aren't willing to be responsible for your own nature and desires. There has got to be a middle road which will make you both happy and it will probably take a lot of giving on both your parts.

Ironic, isn't it? In the beginning, you wanted her because you thought you had finally found a woman that wasn't mean. She was so nice! And she wanted you because she thought you were a lot smarter than you were letting on. Now you find out that you were both wrong.

We men have the hardest time owning up to our basic dumb nature in regard to women. Just lighten up a little bit and accept this premise for a while. I don't mean to encourage you, as a man, to hang on to being dumb about women or use it to justify the dumb things you may do, but it is O.K. to acknowledge that you need to be trained. Just admitting to her how dumb you are makes you one of the smartest dummies around, doesn't it?

HOW TO MAKE SURE THAT YOUR WOMAN ALWAYS FEELS THAT SHE IS WINNING WITH YOU

One of the hardest things I have found for women to put into clear thoughts and communicate is when they don't feel they are winning with a situation or a person, especially a mate.

This situation is one of the most valuable opportunities for her to communicate exactly what she is feeling and what will please her.

You need to be told whenever what you are doing is not working. Of course, she should use the training cycle and not criticize you in a way that makes you feel that you are not competent or able. We men have very large and very, very fragile egos. We want our woman to tell us what she is feeling and what she wants, when we are pleasing her and when we are not. It is a great assistance to us if she keeps her requests simple and easy to do. Even better, she should keep checking in with us to make sure we feel like we are winning and are still willing to give her what she wants.

Our job as men is to keep our women happy. Why? Because there is nothing more beautiful in the whole world than a turned-on and happy woman. If you take care of her, there is very little you cannot accomplish with her help. If you don't take care of her, you will have to drag her with you every step of the way through your life.

Do you get the picture? There you are in lane number three, in the rat race of life with her unhappy, lifeless body hanging over your shoulder. Or worse, she is behind you, hanging on to your belt with her heels dug into the ground and the race is about to begin. It will not be much fun even if you do happen to win whatever race you are in.

On the other hand, she should remember that she is also responsible for her own happiness. Her happiness is not totally up to you. You are not the only option that she has to get what she wants. She has no right to be mean to you, take her anger out on you, or blame you for what she is feeling or when she doesn't get exactly what she wants. If she wants something from you, she needs to make the offer attractive enough for you to want to give it to her. If she really wants something, she will get it.

The second hardest thing for women to ask for directly is attention. I discovered this from being around my wife, Leah, for ten years, and from working with thousands of women while helping them lose weight and get rid of their eating disorders.

Leah would tell me that she wanted attention in every way except with her mouth. She would bump into things, get clumsy, lose things, forget to do something (especially for me), burn food, complain, criticize, sulk, get cranky, irritable, or unreasonable, and in general give me a lot of non-verbal signals that she needed attention.

Being typically dumb about women, I either ignored these signs, tried to fix them, got angry at her, tried to hide from her, or was totally unconscious of what was happening. If I weren't a man or if I were smart about women, I would probably have recognized these as signs that she needed attention. I could have stopped whatever I was doing immediately and put my full attention on her.

I am getting better at recognizing her "signals" for attention. She still has a hard time asking for attention directly. Sometimes she still suppresses what she really wants and does not tell me. Dr. Baranco calls this behavior "ordering short." It means asking for less than is really wanted.

List all the ways you can think of that the women in your life signal their need for attention.

_____

_____

_____

_____

_____

_____

_____●_____

_____

_____

List all the ways that you signal your needs for attention.

_____

_____

_____

_____

_____

_____

THE BOTTOMLESS PIT?

One day I realized that my wife had been wanting attention from me for a very long period of time. I had been very busy and she had not asked for what she wanted in a way that got through to me. She finally accepted the fact that I was not going to read her mind or pick up on any of her subtle signals. She told me as direct as she could that she had needed attention from me for weeks and hadn't gotten any. I asked her what I needed to do to make it up to her.

_____●_____

She said that she wanted my undivided attention for seven straight days. We were on an airplane at the time and I was trying to catch up on a pile of paperwork that I had been carrying around for weeks. I put the papers down and turned my full attention on her.

Nineteen minutes later she felt saturated from all of my attention and could stand it no longer. She told me that it was o.k. with her if I went back to my paperwork. It was as if she were hungry and yet, after a dish or two of exactly what she wanted, she was totally satisfied. Amazing!

Women look insatiable sometimes. It seems like all they want is your twenty-four hours a day, seven days a week, three hundred and sixty five days a year, lifetime attention. It's as if you were being asked to be a captive in solitary confinement for the rest of your life. No wonder we men struggle against it and try every trick we know to avoid giving her what she wants.

The good news is that she only wants attention when she wants it. If you don't give it to her then, you are missing the boat. The best thing you can do is to drop whatever you are doing and flood her with your total attention.

If you have a conflict, explain your problem. You want to give her what she wants immediately, but you have promised to do something else. Let her know you will do whatever she wants. Ask her what you should do. Does she have a solution?

As long as she knows that she is more important to you than your papers or whatever or whoever you are dealing with at the moment, she will help you come up with a solution that is appropriate. Sometimes you need to call someone and reschedule an appointment with them. Sometimes she is willing to let you keep your appointment in return for a date with her at a specific time to give her exactly what she wants.

PRACTICE MAKES PERFECT

We all get a good feeling when we give someone exactly what they want. Basically we like to please each other without injuring ourselves or others if at all possible.

It might be an interesting experiment for you to find out if the same technique of giving non-sexual attention when it is wanted would work on your children, friends, relatives, business associates, and customers.

THE "S" WORD

The third and most difficult thing for a woman to ask her man for is to be pleasured sexually. Something tells me that there is very little difference between the request for attention and this request. Many times the signals are the same . . . except along with her desire to be pleasured sexually comes some variations. Variations such as looking at you with her "sexy look," or putting all her attention just on you, or getting cute and playful. If you ignore these signals or miss their meaning for too long, they will usually turn into snarling and hissing.

Chapter 10

WILL TUMESCENCE BLOW UP
OR SAVE THE WORLD?

———————————•———————————

Maybe this book has the possibility to do far more than the title promises. What if all the women in the world were happy and their men spent all their free time making sure they stayed that way? Wouldn't it be nice if we began to use tumescence for our profit rather than having it control us and make us run around trying to take it out on each other?

I know this is a silly example, but what if it turned out that one hour orgasms were the answer to world peace? They certainly are not expensive, and if they worked, we could cut way down on the defense budget. Our national deficit could be eliminated, not

———————————•———————————

to mention our taxes being lowered.

Sounds far-fetched, doesn't it?

But look at Mikhail Gorbachev and especially the face of his wife, Raisa. Here, most of the time, you see a happy, turned-on woman that seems to be taken care of by her husband. Since he has come to power, great strides have been made toward peace in the world. Raisa looks like she is happy and detumesced and would therefore not be as likely to tumesce Mikhail and make him want to go out and fight with everyone.

On the other hand, do you remember Nikita Krushchev? Did you ever see the expressions on his wife's face? Was this a happy lady? Her face could have been used in the dictionary next to the word "tumesced".

Did she have an effect on her husband? Do you remember Nikita ever acting as if he was tumesced? Has your husband ever taken off his shoe at a business meeting and pounded it on the table?

WHAT DO YOU DO IF SHE IS TUMESCED?

The first thing to do if anyone is tumesced is to recognize and acknowledge it. Once you have identified the real problem, there are many appropriate solutions that will work. You cannot solve any problem in life until you identify the problem accurately. The right solution for the wrong problem will not work.

Tumescence has been misunderstood, run away from, and sedated with illegal and legal drugs. Millions of pounds of chocolate, cheeses, creamy and gooey things, and other greasy foods have been eaten in order to suppress tumescent energy. Billions of cigarettes have been smoked when it has been felt, and tumescent energy has been used in some of the most inefficient and damaging ways anyone could think of, all the way from nail biting and teeth grinding to serious self-mutilation. Now is the time to begin to recognize its potential for pleasure and the productivity that is possible if we tap into this energy source. Let's learn to use tumescence for our profit and pleasure.

1. What are your mate's signals when he/she is tumesced?

_____

_____

_____

_____

_____

_____

2. What words does your mate use to tell you that he/she is tumesced?

_____

_____

_____

_____

_____

3. How do you knowingly upset one another? (What is the recipe that always works? What are the ingredients? The steps?)

_____

_____

_____

_____

_____

_____

HOW DO YOU BECOME TUMESCED OR TUMESCE SOMEONE ELSE?

You can increase tumescence by using any of the five senses, and the sixth sense called conceptual thinking. Any place that you have access to the body's nerve endings are potential areas to directly increase or decrease tumescence.

Touching your mate, where the most nerve endings are available, is the easiest way to control tumescence. Soft touches usually tumesce and increase sexual energy. Heavy pressure usually detumesces and brings the sexual energy down. (The misunderstanding of the desire for detumescence through the use of heavy pressure can lead to wife beating which, of course, is never acceptable.)

Your voice, what you say, or other pleasant sounds such as the ocean, rain, or music can either calm a person if they are too tumesced, or turn them on and raise their sexual energy if they are not tumesced enough. What kind of music or background sounds do you enjoy the most?

_____

_____

_____

_____

_____

———————————————— • ————————————————

_____

_____

Visually, you can use candles or romantic scenes to increase someone's sexual energy. List the visual delights that put you or your mate in a romantic mood?

_____

_____

_____

_____

_____

_____

Pleasant smells are also a turn on. Perfume or other seductive scents make a person feel more turned on. Name some of the fragrances that you or your mate enjoy the most.

_____

_____

_____

———————————————— • ————————————————

_____

_____

_____

Something that tastes wonderful is a sensory treat and puts us in a good frame of mind, and it drives off the not so pleasant feelings of hunger or thirst. List the special foods or drinks that have special romantic meaning for you or your mate._____

_____

_____

_____

Conceptual thought can create fantasies and expectations, which can greatly control someone's tumescent state. Setting out the candles, music, food and otherwise getting the bedroom ready for a "date" can put your mate in a state of expectation. Arranging to spend the weekend at a hotel and talking with anticipation about how much fun you are going to have is a way to build excitement. What ideas to create fantasies and build expectations can you come up with?

_____

_____

_____

WILL TUMESCENCE BLOW UP
OR SAVE THE WORLD

_____
_____
_____
_____
_____
_____
_____

What effect, do you suppose, does pleasing your mate have on their tumescence level?

_____
_____
_____

If you had just experienced a one hour orgasm with your partner, how tumesced do you think you would feel? How irritable?

_____
_____
_____

_____

_____

_____

_____

Can you recall a recent time when you were not sure about how something would turn out or how someone felt about something? Describe the event and how the inability to predict the future affected your tumescent level?

_____

_____

_____

_____

_____

Can you recall a recent time when you were being ignored when you wanted attention? Describe the incident.

_____

_____

_____

———————————————•———————————————

_____

_____

_____

_____

Regarding the above incidents, did you get agitat-ed (tumesced)? Describe your reaction. Did you become angry, moody, jealous, vindictive?

_____

_____

_____

_____

_____

Did you ask for the attention you wanted in an attractive and direct way? What did you say or do?

_____

_____

_____

———————————————•———————————————

_____

_____

_____

_____

What could you have said or done that might have worked and that could have made the person want to give you the attention you needed?

_____

_____

_____

_____

_____

What if you had really enjoyed the amount of attention you were receiving, no matter how small? What effect might that have on the person giving you the attention?

_____

_____

_____

_____

————————————————•————————————————

————————————————————————————————

————————————————————————————————

————————————————————————————————

On the other hand, how does your tumescent level change if someone gives you absolute certainty about something you are worrying about or if they drop everything they are doing and begin to put their total, undivided attention just on you and what you want? Can you recall a time in the past where either of the above occurred? If so, describe what happened and how it made you feel. ——————————

————————————————————————————————

————————————————————————————————

————————————————————————————————

————————————————————————————————

————————————————————————————————

————————————————————————————————

You will begin to see how to use each of the six senses to your advantage as you prepare for your special "Date" which is coming up in Chapter 12.

————————————————•————————————————

WHAT DOES TUMESCENCE WANT?

Tumescence can get you turned on and happier and make you want to have fun until you get enough. It is like anything else. A certain amount is pleasurable, but too much is not. At low levels it feels good. It makes you feel alive, warm, glowing, and tingling with excitement. Your priorities even begin to change. At higher levels it makes you feel off balance, out of sorts, jangled, hot and bothered, frustrated, and wanting to do almost anything that will bring you relief.

WHAT CAN YOU DO WITH TUMESCENCE?

You can learn to use tumescence for your mate's and your own and the world's maximum pleasure. You can bring it down if it is getting too high or raise it up if you want yourself or your partner more excited and turned on. You can learn to build tumescence so that you can give and receive longer and more intense orgasms.

You can choose to use tumescence on purpose or to ignore it. Either way, it is going to express itself one way or the other. Usually, if it is not acknowledged or controlled, it will express itself in some unpleasant way that creates more insanity in the world.

The choice is yours. It will be as if you were standing on the beach knowing that a tidal wave was on the way. If you want, you could ignore it and not try to do anything about it. Or, you can stand there with your surfboard, ready to have some fun. This book is about getting you prepared to know how to surf in a storm and take some great long rides.

My main objective is to begin to make you aware of tumescent energy so you can discover how to spot tumescence and learn how to appropriately deal with it.

Of course, if someone other than your mate is tumesced, you will find the solution is to give them non-sexual attention. Your undivided and sincere attention to what is important to them right now will bring down their tumesced energy faster than almost any other method. If you just show that you care about what they want, and when they want it, you will eventually begin to have a happy person at the other end of your attention.

When it comes to your mate, you usually have the permission and means to give them one of the highest forms of total attention possible, the one hour orgasm. There is very little that can come close to the effect this technique will have on your partner. Your personal worth and self esteem will soar when you master this method. When you walk in a room, you will walk a little taller. People will sense that there is something about you that demands admiration and respect. It is no small feat to be able to produce the kind of result we are talking about in another person and it is something you can be proud of even if no one, other than your mate, knows of your ability.

Other forms of attention are also effective on your mate as well as other people in your life. Paying attention to what they want, when they want it, for as long as they want it, is one of the most considerate and effective things you can do.

Bringing your mate flowers because she deserves to be treated special or giving her a thoughtful gift will make your mate feel that you care about and are thinking about her.

The main thing is to train yourself to become aware of this condition called tumescence and learn how to raise or lower it to create more pleasure and productivity.

Chapter 11

MASTERING COMMUNICATION FOR GREAT SEXING

———————•———————

To master anything, first you must master the language of it. What stops most people from becoming masters with computers is the language. What is DOS? Cursor? RAM? What does "get file" or "copy disk" mean?

Those who get to the other side of these mysteries speak these things as easily as you or I speak English. How do they do it? What is the magic formula?

THEY BEGIN TO SPEAK IT.

It is the same way you learned English. Maybe you called the cat a dog or the dog a cat or mis-

———————•———————

pronounced some word until you were corrected enough and got it right. You just kept making up sounds and saying them out loud.

The more distinctions and differences you can come up with and communicate . . . the more powerful you will be with this part of your life.

DO YOU WANT ME TO RUB ON YOUR WHATCHA-MA-CALL-IT?

Learning the names of the parts of each other's bodies and even the names of the parts of each part will help you as you begin to learn how to pleasure each other.

Later on, I will supply you with a drawing of the sex organs and some names which you will want to become familiar with.

THE MAGIC WORDS TO THE GREATEST SEX YOU'VE EVER HAD

"That's great! Can you . . . come up a little higher?" (move to the left?, press a little harder?, a little softer?, go to the right?, move down a little lower?, go faster?, move a little slower?, stop for a moment?, get me a drink of water?, start again?, move up and down?, go side to side?, use more lubricant?, etc.).

"That's even better. Thank you."

Pretty simple, huh? So why are they magic words? Because they tell your partner exactly what you want and when you want it. If you are the partner, they tell you exactly what you need to be doing and when. Neither of you has to guess or shoot in the dark.

When you know you are going to get what you want, you can relax instead of wondering or hoping and wishing. You will both win instead of trying to figure out if you are doing it "right", or if your partner is going to do it "right."

The acknowledgment at the beginning, "That's great!", lets your partner know they are doing fine. Your partner is winning with you. The acknowledgment at the end, "That's even better" or "That's wonderful. Thank you," lets them know that they are improving and that you appreciate their commitment to pleasing you.

Doesn't everyone like to play a game at which they win? Isn't it fun to keep improving, especially when you get acknowledged for it?

The biggest mistake that people tend to make in this area is to wait too long to communicate. The instant that you want something different than what you are getting, you need to say so immediately.

If you, his wife, wait even thirty seconds to say something, and your husband asks you how long he has been missing the mark and you say thirty seconds, he is going to be upset. You have kept him in mystery for thirty seconds. For thirty seconds you were holding out on him. This kind of behavior begins to break down the trust level between the two of you. You don't trust him enough to tell him the truth and he doesn't trust you to tell him when he is doing well and when he is not.

Do not think that there are other ways to communicate what you want. He cannot read your mind nor can you read his. Your subtle signals like the expression on your face, moving your hip to the left, being quiet, or moaning and groaning can be interpreted in many different ways. This book is not a course in mind reading. It is a course in pleasure. To insure the most pleasure possible, you are going to have to communicate with your mouth.

Although women have in general been taught to communicate more effectively than men with words, they were also taught not to ask for what they really want in the area of sex. In order to have the most pleasure possible, you are going to have to be willing to overcome your reluctance to asking for exactly what you want.

Communicating moment to moment will eventually not be necessary. But during the training cycle of learning how to give each other the ultimate in pleasure, it is critical. If even one stroke goes by with less feeling than the one before, you need to say so right then.

"I didn't feel that last stroke." "The feeling went away." And if I am feeling around for her clitoris, she needs to be willing to tell me, "That isn't it."

The clitoris is sometimes an eccentric little thing and has a tendency to move and hide every once in a while. Unless you TELL HIM that he is not on it, he will not know.

GREAT HELLOS AND GREAT GOOD-BYES

One of the most effective things you can do to improve your relationship with your wife or husband or even the people you work with is to GIVE THEM GREAT HELLOS AND GREAT GOOD-BYES.

How many times have you come home, maybe grunted something barely understandable, pecked your mate on the cheek, and started complaining about how miserable your day has been?

Have you ever been in such a hurry when you were leaving that all you did was to toss her a "Bye" before you ran out the door?

This is one of the major areas which begins to take the excitement out of a relationship. You start to take each other for granted. You fall into a rut and with every passing day it gets dug deeper and deeper.

Remember our dog analogy? Let's use him again. Have you ever noticed how dogs ALWAYS give great hellos and great good-byes? You could have been gone for a couple of hours and you get the same greeting as you would if they hadn't seen you in a week.

And how about when you leave? Do they let you know they would like to go with you and are sad that you are leaving? Isn't it great?

Here is your assignment if you choose to accept it. For the next week, give each other great hellos and great good-byes, no matter what. No matter how late you are, no matter how tumesced you are, no matter anything. Just drop everything else and do it with full-out enthusiasm. Keep thinking about what the dog would do under the same circumstances.

Can you imagine how much fun it is going to be for your man to come home and find you wagging your tail, ready to jump into his arms and smother him with kisses? How great is it going to make him feel when you give him a great good-bye and let him know that you don't want him to leave and that you wish you could go with him? Wouldn't that make anyone eager to come back home to get more of that kind of attention?

Chapter 12

SETTING UP
THE SPECIAL "DATE"

Now you are ready to begin to work on giving and receiving one hour orgasms. The whole process actually begins long before you physically touch your partner.

To accomplish the intensity, duration, and pleasure of orgasm that we are looking for, it is mandatory that both of you put your total attention on just one of you at a time.

For the beginning step, you must decide who is going to go first. Usually, the woman should be the first to be taken on the "Date."

(This will probably be different if the woman reads this book first and fears that her mate may resist too much if she tries to get him to read or apply it. In that case, read the suggestion to the first question in Chapter 14.)

To start, tell your mate that you are taking her on a special date and when the date is going to begin. Your job here is to tell her in such a way as to begin to get her excited (positively tumesced). Make sure you have her undivided attention when you tell her about the date.

Next, if the date is far enough off, begin to leave her love notes so she will get more and more excited about the date. Put the notes where she will stumble across them, such as on the refrigerator door or on her pillow. You can mail her a romantic card or note in the mail. Even send or leave her small presents or flowers with a card attached. How about an unexpected phone call just to say how much you love her and how much you are looking forward to your date?

The note could say something like, "Our date will be one that you will never forget." "I'm going to take you to heights you have never been to before," or, "Remember, our date is only a few hours away." You can even remind her of a special moment you once shared and tell her this time is going to be even better. Thank her for something she has done for you or tell her what she means to you.

CHECKLIST?

Prior to the time of the date, make sure that all the details are taken care of: music, candles, something to drink and munch on. Make sure the room is perfect, that your fingernails have been manicured so that they are rounded with no sharp edges.

Make a checklist so you don't leave anything out. This makes it easier for you to pull everything together. Start your list now and add to it as you think of more items. Write down everything you need to do and the time it needs to be done.

As the date progresses, you will most likely run into a few snags or even some resistance. Just include everything that happens as part of the process of getting her tumesced.

For example, she may be preoccupied with something else that is going on in her life and may start treating the date with something less than wide-eyed excitement. In that case, it may be a good idea to tease her by talking about taking it away from her. Don't do this in a heavy-handed way or else she may blow up at you and dig her heels in. There is nothing worse than trying to deal with a mind that has already make a decision. Stay light about it.

The main thing is for you to stay in charge and totally confident that everything will happen when you are ready. You need not force or hurry anything. Just let events unfold at their own pace, even if it means slowing things down so that you do not feel rushed or pressured. But, once you have promised the date, you must go through with it no matter what.

For this "date" to work, you must put her at "total effect," which means that you are the "doer" and she is being "done" with no effort or energy on her part whatsoever. It is your job to stop her if she tries to help at any point during the process. You handle all decisions, baby-sitters, phone calls, emergencies, and everything else that comes up in a way that you know will please her.

DO YOUR HOMEWORK

You will also need to do your homework which will involve completing this chapter and reading the sections in Chapter 7 that apply to your partner. Read the part entitled either "WOMEN ONLY" or "MEN ONLY" as it applies to your partner. Become very familiar with the body parts which are described in these sections. Pay special attention to the individual parts of your partner's genitals. Get to know them and their names as well as you do the parts of your own body.

Begin to anticipate the amount and kind of touching each part of your partner's genitals will respond to. This is not nearly as complicated as you may think. A woman's clitoris is very similar to the shaft of a man's penis and its end, the clitoral glans, is like the crown or end of a man's penis. The hood of the clitoris is like his foreskin. You can think of the penis as a large clitoris and the clitoris as a small penis.

BUILDING TUMESCENCE

As we have up to this point, we are going to proceed as if the man is taking the woman on the "date." On some future "date," when the roles reverse, just change the following instructions to fit the situation.

Your job is to begin to build and take control of her tumescence. This will begin right after you make the "date" and will continue right up to the time the "date" ends. It could start out or include bringing or sending her some flowers (men like flowers too) and even taking her on a shopping trip to buy her a small gift or some clothing or sexy lingerie for your "date." It usually is very effective to fix her a romantic meal or take her to a special restaurant just before the "date."

HOW TO "DO" YOUR PARTNER TO CREATE THE MOST INTENSE AND PLEASURABLE ORGASMIC STATE POSSIBLE

It is time to make your move. You will now begin

to move all the excitement you have been building in her brain down into her crotch area. The easiest way to do this is to directly stimulate the nerve endings of her body. Go very slowly. Start by kissing her softly in a way that lets her know you are in charge. Do not let her kiss you back unless you want her to. You are the kisser. She is being done.

When you are ready and you have the bedroom ready, take her there and begin to slowly remove her clothes. Talk to her sweetly as you are doing this by telling her all the things that turn you on and what you love about her skin and her body. Another idea would be to undress her in complete silence and forbid her to say anything. Do what feels good to you and it will almost always be pleasurable to your mate.

When you are finished undressing her, you may want to give her a sensual bath. If you do, make sure it was on your checklist and is already set up and ready.

You can be undressed also or you could even be wearing a tuxedo or a pirate suit. Do whatever is going to be fun for you. Undressing slowly to music in front of her might increase the suspense and tumescence you are attempting to build.

Afterwards, you will dry her off with towels which could even be scented with a fragrance she likes and may even have been warmed in the oven.

(Note: Be careful. Do not put the towels in the oven when it is on. Setting the house on fire may alter the plans for your special evening. Turn the oven on warm; after it has warmed up, shut it off. Check the oven to make sure it is not too hot, and then put the towels in the oven on a rack away from the burners. Let them stay there until you are ready for them.)

Take her to a bed and tell her to lie down on her back. Make sure she is comfortable and warm. You can cover her with a sheet or warm dry towels. Take off your rings and jewelry. Put some Vaseline or a body lotion in your hands and warm it up by rubbing your hands together before applying it to her body. Whatever she is lying on is going to get oil on it, so you may want to put towels under the sheet or have her lie directly on the towels.

Start with her feet. Remember to take "taking touches" as you did when you were doing yourself during "tactile inventory." If it feels good to your hand, it will probably feel good to her.

All the way through this process allow yourself to feel the good feelings that she is experiencing. It is as if you were touching her and feeling what she is feeling at the same time in your own body. This is going to be very important to both of you, especially when you get to the groin area.

As you are touching her and moving from one area

to another, make sure you are staying in communication with her. Do this from the very beginning of the "date". TELL HER WHAT YOU ARE GOING TO DO BEFORE YOU DO IT AND GET FEEDBACK FROM HER AS YOU GO ALONG AS TO WHAT FEELS THE BEST.

If you need to stop to put some more oil or Vaseline on your hands, let her know BEFORE you stop. When you are warming the oil up in your hands, say, "I'm warming the oil up in my hands before I put it on you. . . Now it's warm enough and I'm going to spread it on your skin." Inform her of what you are doing step by step so she doesn't have to think or try to figure it out. There is no need to tell her anything except what the next step is.

The feet are very sensitive and have a lot of nerve endings that can give great pleasure. Women have reported having orgasms from just having their feet rubbed. Tell her this and let her know that you won't take her that far this time, while you are working on her feet, but she can still enjoy it as much as she wants.

Try stroking the arch of the foot back and forth from the ball of the foot to the heel. Also, try the middle toe of each foot. Many people feel stimulation in their clitoris or penis when these areas are rubbed. Press in and stroke hard enough to give her pleasure, but not too hard as to cause pain or too light as to tickle. All through the massage try to find just the right touch by talking to her and having her tell you what feels best to her.

Next, take her hand and begin to work on her fingers, working up her hands, then arms, and on to the front of her shoulders and her chest. Begin to make circles around the outermost rim of her breasts. Be careful not to touch the nipples. They may be too sensitive and cause her pain if you touch them directly or before they are ready.

Slowly begin to make the circles smaller and smaller as if you are teasing the nipples. Make them want to be touched. When you think they are ready and she is expecting them to be touched, tell her that you are now going to go back to rubbing the outside rim of her breasts and do so.

Keep repeating this process of teasing until you have increased her tumescence up to a point that you are ready to touch them. Some people have very sensitive nipples and you should use a lot of lubricant. You may even need to put a piece of thin cloth over her and touch the nipples through the cloth. The main thing is to touch them in a way that gives her the most pleasure.

When this area has had enough, begin to work on the fronts of the thighs and the stomach. The rectus muscles in the stomach look like two wide rubber bands which run from the bottom of the rib cage down to the top of the groin area. These muscles will sometimes stand up as high as two inches when a very thin woman is feeling pleasure from being touched.

Remember, tell her what you are going to do and have her tell you what kind of touching feels best to her. Continue to touch that area until you are tired of touching it and then TELL HER YOU ARE MOVING ON TO ANOTHER AREA.

When you have done these areas, you can begin to start making circles slowly around her groin area with your hand. Begin to tease the groin section. When you are ready, tell her to spread her legs so that you can apply Vaseline to her. Warm it up with your hands and start on the area around the vaginal opening. As you are doing this, ask her to spread her fingers and toes and to feel what you are doing to her all the way out to those areas. Many women and men report that when they do this, it allows them to feel pleasurable feelings more intensely.

Use a lot of Vaseline. Vaseline prevents injury from long periods of friction and you can use both heavy or light pressure. It is not water soluble, so even perspiration will not wash it off. Vaseline also spreads and radiates the pleasurable sensations to other nearby parts. Vaseline seems to have a consistency that is preferable to other brands even though it is made of basically the same ingredients. After this first date you can try other brands, if you like, to see which one you prefer.

Remember to keep talking to her. Tell her what you are doing and keep asking for feedback.

Begin to spread the Vaseline on the outer lips of her vagina (labia majora), then the inner lips (labia minora), then the opening to the vagina. Finally, follow the inner lips up to the point that they begin to form the hood over the clitoris. Carefully begin to lubricate the hood of the clitoris and very gently include the head of the clitoris (clitoral glans) itself.

As the skin begins to become swollen with blood from increased circulation and excitement, you may notice that the hairs around the vagina become erect and the lips around the vagina open up by themselves. The hairs are an extension of the skin. Run your hand over the tops of the hairs, touching them lightly and ask your partner if she feels a pleasurable sensation from that being done to her.

PICTURE OF FEMALE GROIN AREA

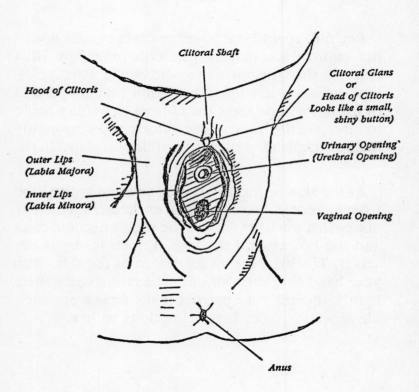

Clitoral Shaft

Clitoral Glans
or
Head of Clitoris
Looks like a small,
shiny button)

Hood of Clitoris

Urinary Opening
(Urethral Opening)

Outer Lips
(Labia Majora)

Inner Lips
(Labia Minora)

Vaginal Opening

Anus

At this point you need to decide what position would be most comfortable for you. It is important that you are comfortable during this entire process. If you are not, your partner will pick up your stress and it will decrease the amount of pleasure you both are having.

MASTER THE POSSIBILITIES

The basic decision you need to make is whether you will use both hands or just one. There are many positions a man can use while he is doing a woman. We will talk about a few of the possibilities and you can select the one which works best for you.

If you use the two-hand position, you can start out on whichever side of her is the most comfortable for you. Slide your hand that is nearest her feet under her buttocks. Your thumb can rest lightly on her vaginal opening and your middle or index finger near or on her anus. Later on in the process you may feel your fingers being sucked in to one or both of her openings. Until then, do not attempt to press your fingers inside of her. Just let them rest gently on the outside. Some people use a single-use examination glove on one or both hands. Do whatever is the most appropriate for you. The use of examination gloves is discussed more fully in Chapter 13.

Try out three or more of these positions and a couple of others that you make up. Have fun while deciding which position to use. The main concern is that you are comfortable.

1. KNEELING BESIDE HER: Approach her from whichever side you wish. This position may become tiresome after a while and begin to hurt your knees, but, it allows you to keep eye contact and talk to her easily.

2. SITTING BESIDE HER WITH ONE LEG OVER HER STOMACH AND THE OTHER UNDER HER LEGS: In this position you may find it necessary to prop yourself up with pillows or lean your back against the headboard or a wall next to the bed.

3. LIE BESIDE HER WITH YOUR HEAD TOWARD HER FEET. ONE ARM IS OVER HER LEG, HOLDING YOURSELF UP ON YOUR ELBOW: Using this position, you can easily use both hands as well as see what you are doing. You will usually be stimulating the clitoris using the hand of the arm on which you are leaning. Use your top hand to anchor the clitoris in place with your thumb or by using both your middle and index finger on either side of the clitoris.

These next positions are for a one handed approach.

1. LIE BESIDE HER WITH ONE ARM UNDER HER NECK AND OVER HER OPPOSITE SHOULDER SO YOU CAN REACH HER BREAST: Your other arm reaches straight down to her crotch.

2. LIE BESIDE HER WHILE PROPPING YOUR HEAD OR BODY UP WITH ONE ARM: Your other arm reaches straight down to her crotch.

3. LIE BESIDE HER WITH HER ARM AROUND YOU AND WITH YOUR HEAD ON HER CHEST: Your arm reaches straight down to her crotch.

4. LIE BESIDE HER WITH YOUR HEAD TOWARD HER FEET. ONE ARM IS OVER HER LEG, HOLDING YOURSELF UP ON YOUR ELBOW.

Once you are in a comfortable position, use your free hand to begin to "take" pleasuring strokes. Don't start at the focal point, the clitoris, but instead begin at the outermost part of an imaginary circle far from the clitoris and begin to work your way toward it.

You are attempting to tumesce the clitoris. Make it want to be touched. Tease it as long as possible before you finally begin to give it any direct pleasure.

You can start with the hairs of the vagina, then work down to the outer lips, then the inner lips, to the opening of the vagina, and finally directly up from the vagina opening to the middle ridge, which is the clitoris.

Wring out every bit of pleasure you can from each part before going on to the next. Talking to her as you go along can help to turn her on. Keep saying romantic things to her that get her more and more excited. Tell her how beautiful, radiant, and exciting she is and threaten not to stop until the sun comes up. Let her know you could touch her this way all night long. Talk about how much the specific parts you are working on are enjoying what you are doing to them.

Women love to be told over and over how much they turn you on and how beautiful they are. They never get tired of hearing compliments, anymore than you get tired of being told how well you did when you accomplished something.

When you find the clitoris, you can anchor the hood back by using your thumb with your fingers pointing down toward her vaginal opening. With your index or middle finger you can begin to find the area on or around the clitoris which gives her the most pleasure. Most women will have more feeling on one side of their clitoris than on the other. Sometimes, until she is very excited, the head of the clitoris is too sensitive to stimulate directly. Have her tell you where to stroke that feels the best to her.

On some women, the clitoris is hard to find and stay in contact with. It might keep slipping away from you. Don't worry or let her get upset. You are just one step away from finding it. Stay in communication with her so that you know you are still on the right spot. If you get off the right spot for even one stroke, let her know that you want her to say so immediately. An easy way to find the clitoris is to start at the vaginal opening and go straight up until you feel a bump. That's it.

Start out with an up and down movement, the bread and butter stroke, and as you feel her tumescence begin to build up to a critical point, either change the stroke to side to side or lighten the pressure you are using or stop altogether. Remember, tell her what you are going to do before you do it.

She may beg you to let her go over the top, but do not do this until you are ready for her to go. Tell her over and over that everything will be all right, just relax and maybe next time you will let her go. Slow her down. Don't rush. You have all night if you want.

Hold out as long as possible. You can switch to rubbing on her outer or inner lips. It will be pleasurable, but she will probably want you back on the clitoris as quickly as possible. Don't let her rush you. You are in charge and will get her there in due time.

Now would be a good time to "connect up" other parts of her body with her clitoris. The instructions, on how to do this "connection" exercise, are in the homework which asked you to read her "tactile inventory" process. Basically, you are to rub on some part of her body which contains a large number of nerve endings and create a sympathetic response in her clitoris.

An example would be her breasts. Tell her you are going to begin to rub on her breast at the same time you are stroking her clitoris. Once she is feeling pleasurable sensations in both areas, tell her that you are going to stop rubbing on her clitoris, but you want her to "feel" the touching you are doing to her breast or nipple in her clitoris. Get feedback and after a while, inform her that you are switching back to her clitoris. Now you want her to feel your touching on her clitoris in her nipples. Keep going back and forth until you have set up a connection between the two. Stop whenever you get tired of doing this.

The most common areas that seem to lend themselves favorably to being connected are the areas used in petting such as her neck, lips, stomach, the inside of her legs, her knees, as well as her breasts and nipples. Other areas with large amounts of nerve endings such as the middle toe, the anus, and just inside the vagina opening can also be explored.

One inch of penetration inside the vagina can be felt by her as far up as 12 inches or more. Also, if you reach inside of her and press against the vaginal wall at the 3, 6, 9, and 12 o'clock positions, you may find sensitive areas which she may like you to rub. The 12 o'clock position is interesting because it is directly behind her clitoris and enables you to give her the feeling that you are stimulating the clitoris from the rear. This area, which is about the size of a button and gets hard as the woman gets excited, is sometimes referred to as the G-Spot. It is sometimes too sensitive to touch except when the woman is highly aroused and close to climaxing.

OVER THE TOP

At some point you will be ready to take her over the top. You will have been keeping her in an orgasmic state as close to peaking her as you have wanted to. Remember to tell her what you are going to do before you do it. You might even use this opportunity to peak her some more.

Sometimes, you can play with her in a way that increases her tumescence. Tell her that, just for fun, she has only twenty seconds to go over the top and if she doesn't make it you are going to bring her down one more time. She will probably choke up under the pressure and not make it. Good! Every time you peak her, you build up the pressure of the climax and take it to a level that would not have been possible without peaking.

If you are feeling charitable, you might give her a whole thirty seconds to go over the top the next time you start to bring her to the edge.

Once she starts over the top, stay very alert to what you are feeling in your finger. It is usually time for you to begin to lighten the pressure or else her climax could turn from pleasure to pain. Give her just enough pressure, but not too much. You will learn as you practice how much feels the best and when to begin to lighten your stroke. You will notice that she will pull away from you when you are pressing too hard and push toward you when she wants more pressure.

Here's the best part. Once she has climaxed totally and has nothing left, there are still pleasurable feelings left over for the taking. All you need to do is
to continue to stroke her, using more Vaseline if
necessary, using a lighter and lighter touch as you
bring her down. Your job here is to bring her all the
way down and not leave her feeling like she is floating three feet over the bed. She will probably never
have had this done to her before, but you will know
you are finished when she is totally "flat." This
means there are no more pleasurable sensations left
in her.

You still are not finished. She is probably not all
of the way detumesced. This means, using our scale
of tumescent energy, she would not be at a level one
yet. A good way to end with her is to lie on top of
her. Heavy pressure on her body, her chest, or head
will help bring her completely down.

At this point, if you have been allowing yourself
to feel what she has been feeling, you may feel as
if you have gone through the orgasmic state and climax yourself and feel totally detumesced.

After your partner is totally "flat," have her tell
you everything about how the whole "date" was for
her from beginning to end. Have her especially go
into detail and be specific as to what pleasurably sensitive areas you discovered.

Don't let up at this point. You are still in the process of making love to each other. Being intimate and

talking is just as much a part of lovemaking as is touching. You will be amazed at how much you continue to discover about each other and how new and exciting being with each other will become.

Well? Did you keep time? Did you make it for one hour this session?

Don't worry. Keep practicing and you will eventually get there. The truth is, it doesn't make much difference, does it? The idea is not how long you can sustain an orgasmic state. It is not even how intense or long the climax is. The most important goal is to see how much pleasure both of you can get out of practicing this method. Each time you do, you will find yourself going for more and more pleasure.

Although it is not hard being patient when you are having fun, begin to think of training for your one hour orgasm as if you were training to run a marathon. You would not jump up the first day and run 26 miles as hard as you could. You would start out with a mile or two at a slow pace. Later you would increase your distance until you got up to your goal. The same is true in learning this technique. Practice with each other every chance you get and make it as much fun as you can.

The information you have received so far is adequate to eventually produce a one hour orgasmic state. We have seen a video demonstration of one of Dr. Baranco's faculty having orgasmic contractions for an hour. I have also interviewed many people who have achieved this goal, however, one hour orgasms are not the primary purpose of this work. It is a side benefit.

THE MAIN PURPOSE OF THE WORK OF DR. BARANCO IS TO TEACH PEOPLE HOW TO HAVE RELATIONSHIPS THAT WORK AND TO GET MORE PLEASURE OUT OF THEIR RELATIONSHIPS AND THEIR LIVES.

Good luck and have lots of fun.

DOING YOUR MAN

WOMEN'S POSITIONS

1. KNEEL OR SIT BETWEEN THE MAN'S LEGS, FACING HIS CROTCH. Your legs can either be under or inside his legs.

2. LIE BETWEEN HIS LEGS WITH YOUR HEAD ON HIS THIGH AND HIS OTHER LEG OVER YOUR BODY.

3. KNEEL OR SIT WITH YOUR LEGS CROSSED BESIDE HIM.

4. LIE WITH HIS ARM AROUND YOU AND WITH YOUR HEAD RESTING ON HIS CHEST: Your top arm reaches straight down to his crotch.

5. SITTING BESIDE HIM WITH ONE LEG OVER HIS STOMACH AND THE OTHER UNDER HIS LEGS: In this position you may find it necessary to prop yourself up with pillows or lean your back against the headboard or a wall next to the bed.

Once you are in a comfortable position, use your free hand to begin to "take" pleasuring strokes. Don't start on the focal point, the penis, but instead begin at the outermost part of a circle around the penis and begin to work your way in toward it.

You are attempting to tumesce his penis. Make it want to be touched. Tease it as long as possible before you finally begin to give it any direct pleasure.

The hairs are an extension of the skin. Run your hand over the tops of the hairs, touching them lightly and ask your partner if he gets a pleasurable sensation from this being done to him. Try tickling strokes from your fingernails on his lower stomach.

As the area around the groin begins to become swollen with blood from increased circulation and excitement, you may notice that the hairs around the penis begin to stand up.

PICTURE OF THE PENIS AREA

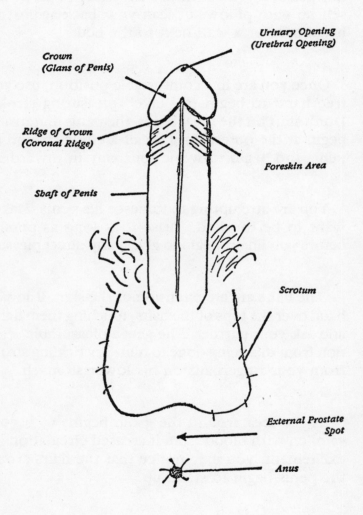

Crown
(Glans of Penis)

Urinary Opening
(Urethral Opening)

Ridge of Crown
(Coronal Ridge)

Foreskin Area

Shaft of Penis

Scrotum

External Prostate
Spot

Anus

When you are ready, start applying Vaseline to his scrotum (the sack that covers his testicles). Be very careful. Do not push upwards because this can be very painful. Continue to apply Vaseline until you have covered his penis and the areas around it.

Keep asking him how what you are doing feels to him and if you are hurting him at all? Talking to him as you go along can help to turn him on and make it easier for him to surrender to you. Keep saying romantic things to him that get him more and more excited. Tell him how exciting it is for you to be doing this and threaten not to stop until you make him late for work the next day or his next appointment. Let him know you could touch him this way all night long. Talk about how much the specific parts you are working on are enjoying what you are doing to them. Keep getting feedback on what feels the best to him.

Start out with his penis, using an up and down movement. As you feel his tumescence begin to build up, either change the stroke or lighten the pressure you are using or stop all together. Remember, tell him what you are doing before you do it.

Begin to explore different parts and the sides of his penis. Alter the kind of strokes you use. The most sensitive parts of his penis will usually be the ridge of the crown and the area on the bottom side of the base of the crown. Also check how pleasurable it feels to him to be stroked in different directions at different speeds and pressures.

He may beg you to let him go over the top, but do not do this until you are ready for him to go. Tell him over and over that everything will be all right, just relax and maybe next time you will turn him loose.

Hold out as long as possible. You can switch to rubbing different parts of his penis. It will be pleasurable, but he will probably want you back on the most sensitive and pleasurable part of the penis as quickly as possible. Don't let him rush you. You are in charge and will get him there in due time.

Now would probably be a good time to try to "connect up" other parts of his body with his penis. The instructions for this are in your homework which asked you to read his "tactile inventory" process. Basically, you are to rub on some part of his body which contains a large number of nerve endings and create a sympathetic response in his penis.

An example would be his chest. Tell him you are going to begin to rub on his chest at the same time you are stroking his penis. Once he is feeling pleasurable sensations in both areas, tell him that you are going to stop rubbing on his penis, but you want him to see if he can "feel" your touching of his chest or nipples also in his penis. After a while, inform him that you are switching back to his penis and now you want him to feel your touching of his penis in his chest. Keep going back and forth until you have set up a connection between the two or whenever you get tired of doing this.

The most common areas that seem to lend themselves favorably to being connected are the areas used in petting such as his neck, lips, inside the mouth, his stomach, the inside of his legs, as well as his chest and nipples. Other areas with large amounts of nerve endings such as the middle toe and the area around the anus can also be explored.

OVER THE TOP

At some point you will be ready to take him over the top. You will have been keeping him in an orgasmic state as close to peaking him as you have wanted to. Remember to tell him what you are going to do before you do it. You might even use this opportunity to "peak" him some more.

Sometimes, you can play with him in a way that increases his tumescence. Tell him that he has only twenty seconds to go over the top and if he doesn't make it, you are going to bring him down one more time. He will probably choke up under the pressure and not make it. Good! Every time you "peak" him, you build up the pressure of the climax and take it to a level that would not have been possible without peaking.

If you are feeling charitable, you might give him a whole thirty seconds to go over the top the next time you start to bring him to the edge.

Once he starts over the top, stay very alert to what you are feeling in your hand. You may need to begin either to lighten or increase the pressure you are using. Give him just enough pressure, but not too much. You will learn as you practice how much feels the best and when to begin to lighten or increase your stroke. You will notice that he will pull away from you if you are pressing too hard and push toward you if he wants more pressure.

Here's the best part. Once he has climaxed totally and has nothing left, there are still pleasurable feelings left over for the taking. All you need to do is to continue to stroke him, using more Vaseline if necessary and a lighter and lighter touch as you bring him down. Your job here is to bring him all of the way down and not leave him feeling like he is floating three feet over the bed. You will know you are finished when he is totally "flat." This means there are no more pleasurable sensations left in him.

You still are not finished. He is probably not all of the way detumesced. A good way to end with him is to lie on top of him. Heavy pressure on his body, his chest, or head will help bring him down.

At this point, if you have been allowing yourself to feel what he has been feeling, you may feel as if you have gone through the orgasmic state and climax yourself and feel totally detumesced.

After your partner is totally "flat," have him tell you everything about how the whole "date" was for him from beginning to end. Have him especially go into detail and be specific as to what pleasurably sensitive areas you discovered.

Don't let up at this point. You are still in the process of making love to each other. Being intimate and talking is just as much a part of lovemaking as is touching each other. You will be amazed at how much you continue to discover about each other and how new and exciting being with each other will become.

Well? Did you keep time? Did you make it for one hour this session?

Don't worry. Keep practicing and you will eventually get there. The truth is, it doesn't make much difference, does it? The idea is not how long you can sustain an orgasmic state. It is not even how intense or long the climax is. You may even go past the point of orgasm sometimes and miss the mark. In the long run, it doesn't matter. The most important goal is to see how much pleasure both of you can get out of using this method. Each time you do it you will find yourself going for more and more pleasure.

Although it is not hard being patient when you are having fun, begin to think of training for your one hour orgasm as if you were training to run a marathon. You would not jump up the first day and run 26 miles as hard as you could. You would start out with a mile or two at a slow pace. Later you would increase your distance until you got up to your goal. The same is true in learning this technique. Practice with each other every chance you get and make it as much fun as you can.

The information you have received so far is adequate to eventually produce a one hour orgasmic state. We have seen a video demonstration of one of Dr. Baranco's faculty having orgasmic contractions for an hour. I have also interviewed many people who have achieved this goal, however, one hour orgasms are not the primary purpose of this work. It is a side benefit.

THE MAIN PURPOSE OF THE WORK OF DR. BARANCO IS TO TEACH PEOPLE HOW TO HAVE RELATIONSHIPS THAT WORK AND TO GET MORE PLEASURE OUT OF THEIR RELATIONSHIPS AND THEIR LIVES.

Good luck and have lots of fun.

Chapter 13

SINGLE AND GETTING READY FOR A COMMITTED RELATIONSHIP

───────────────●───────────────

There are other benefits in this book that should not be overlooked. If you are single, it could help you find the relationship you are looking for and it could save your life.

If you are single and looking for a committed relationship, there is a premise I would like you to consider. It is the presumption that it is the WOMAN that chooses the MAN. Check it out, as I did, by interviewing single men and women and see if it holds up.

───────────────●───────────────

One of the problems with this theory is that most men still like to believe that they are the ones that are doing the choosing.

But wouldn't it be nice if what I just proposed was the way everyone thought of it? If you were a man, you would just go around practicing putting all of your attention on every available woman that you came in contact with. You would let women know that you are trainable and appreciate any training they are willing to give you.

If you are a woman, you could practice every chance you get with every prospective man that came along. Without having sex with him you could practice training him by using the training cycle described in chapter 8. Work on some nonsexual behavior of his that you would like to change. Just have him win with you in a way that is fun for him. Make him feel good about being around you. Broadcast your happy and turned-on energy to him every chance you get.

Needless to say, you cannot practice if you lock yourself in your home. You need to get yourself to a place where there are eligible people for you to consider.

I have two suggestions other than the ones you have probably already heard, such as church, ski clubs, and computer clubs. One of the fastest growing ways to meet the perfect person is to look into video dating services. They are incredible. It is like having been on a diet and then suddenly being turned loose in a candy store.

You get to look through albums and albums full of other single men or women who are also looking for a relationship. Also, you get to "meet" the person and listen to them by watching a video made while they are being professionally interviewed. The interview shows what they are really like and what they are looking for in someone else.

If you, a woman, feels an attraction or an interest in one of the men, a postcard is sent, letting him know that you would like to meet him. If that individual hasn't yet found the right person, he comes in and watches your video and gets to know what you are like and what you are looking for in a relationship. If that person also feels an attraction and interest in you, you are put in touch with each other. You call and talk and if all goes well, you set up a meeting over coffee.

It is like going out on your sixth date because you already know a great deal about each other, and especially you know that you already like each other. The worst thing that can happen is that when the other person gets the postcard saying someone is interested in him, he will already be working on another relationship or he will not be as interested in you as you are in him. If the latter happens, it is a painless rejection. You simply do not hear from him.

The second most effective way to meet other people is to do volunteer work for some worthy organization, ideally, an organization in which your communication and presentation skills are brought out and encouraged. If you would like a list of suggested organizations in your area, send me a self-addressed and stamped envelope to:

BREAKTHRU PUBLISHING
P.O.BOX 2866,
HOUSTON, TEXAS 77252-2866.

SAFE SEX

What you are about to be taught will not only bring pleasure to you and your future partner beyond your wildest dreams, it is also the answer to "Survival Sex." Dr. Baranco says that "safe" sex may not be adequate. He goes far beyond the methods being suggested at this time and has come up with methods which are not only sensuous and pleasurable, but are also as careful as anyone can devise without total abstinence.

The "Survival Sex" practices are designed for anyone who has a partner who has had "intimate contact" with someone else within a five-to ten-year period. "Intimate contact" is any circumstance where there was or might have been an exchange of body fluids, whether through sexual contact or not: blood transfusions, intercourse, oral sex, deep kissing, or needles.

In some cases AIDS can be transmitted if a person has a cut (even one invisible to the naked eye), a rash, an abrasion, a broken blister or some other opening or weakness in the skin's epidermal barrier, and is then exposed to infected blood or other body fluids.

In order to be really safe, an AIDS test should be done now and another done six months from now. During the six-month testing period, "Survival Sex" should be practiced. After the second successful AIDS test, it is safe, as can now be determined, to stop using the "Survival Sex" practices as long as you continue to stay monogamous and free of any other kind of intimate contact.

In Dr. William Masters and Virginia Johnson's recent book, *CRISIS: Heterosexual Behavior in the Age of AIDS*, they talk about the potential for the AIDS disease to spread throughout the heterosexual community in epidemic proportions. In reading about their research on the subject, it is easy to become alarmed about how lightly most of the heterosexual community is taking this threat to their lives.

Masters and Johnson believe that authorities are greatly underestimating the number of people infected with the AIDS virus in the population today. Six out of every hundred heterosexual people in their study came down with the AIDS virus.

If 6 out of every 100 airplanes crashed, most of us would not fly. Even though their research was limited to a narrow group of heterosexuals who had multiple partners, it seems unreasonably dangerous and reckless not to exhibit some realistic caution and common sense.

Most people who have the AIDS virus and transmit it to others are otherwise healthy and don't realize they are infected. Many of them do not take any precautions in terms of sexual behavior, so they continue to pass the AIDS virus along.

According to Masters and Johnson, the indications are that the AIDS virus is even working its way into the younger population—the 15 to 24 age group—which has, at least in the last quarter century, been the primary force driving epidemics of sexually transmitted diseases in the world.

If you are still not certain that you are committed to protecting yourself and others from the spread of AIDS, I seriously recommend that you invest the time to read every page of *CRISIS: Heterosexual Behavior in the Age of AIDS*.

SENSUOUS "SURVIVAL SEX"

Sensuous "Survival Sex" begins with getting prepared so that you and your partner will be as safe as you possibly can be without abstaining from sexing altogether.

The formula for Sensual "Survival Sex" is:

1. A substance that kills the AIDS virus

2. A barrier

3. A substance that kills the AIDS virus

This means that first you apply the prescribed amount of the creams or jellies which contain nonoxynol-9, the active ingredient which is known to kill the AIDS virus. Follow the instructions on the label and make sure that you cover any part of you which will be touching your partner. Your lips, hands, inside your mouth, your genitals.

Second, slip into a pair of disposable vinyl examination gloves that doctors use. These are available in different sizes at your local drugstore. Make that snapping noise when you are putting them on so that your partner will begin to associate the sound to mean that "pleasure is on its way."

Last, put another coating of the cream or jelly that contains nonoxynol-9 over the entire surface of the glove and then begin to apply it to the areas of your partner which you are going to touch.

If you are going to engage in intercourse, use the same method of putting the nonoxynol-9 over the penis and surrounding areas as well as inside and all around the outside of the vagina. Next, put on a latex condom and then put the nonoxynol-9 over the outside of it. Do not use "natural material" condoms, made of animal intestines. They are designed to prevent pregnancy, but viruses, such as AIDS, can sneak through.

If you are going to practice oral sex on a woman, Dr. Baranco has come up with a new use for Saran Wrap which I do not think is listed as one of the possibilities on the box. You follow the same formula as above. Put nonoxynol-9 on any area of your body which is going to come into contact with her body, as well as that area you will be touching on her body. Then lay a sheet of Saran Wrap over her clitoral area. Now you are ready to stimulate her clitoris orally.

Additional warning: Vaseline and other petroleum jellies contain properties which will destroy the material that the disposable gloves are made of. Although Vaseline is the preferred lubricant, you have to use a non-petroleum type lubricant to keep any friction from hurting your partner.

One of the problems in the past with prevention methods is that we have had to apply them as quickly as possible after we had become aroused and they were seen as a delay to pleasuring ourselves or our partners.

Practicing the technique of *THE ONE HOUR ORGASM* gives you all the time in the world to get ready. If you are a man and your partner knows that you are getting ready to pleasure her while she is lying on the bed in anticipation, everything you do that gets you closer to starting will add to her tumescent state. Your preparations can become a part of turning on your partner, as well as letting her know that you care enough about her to take precautions which could save her life.

Six months is not a long time to practice "Survival Sex," especially when the only alternative is to put your life at risk. It is also a strong incentive to have a lifetime monogamous relationship with a partner who is trained to give you all the pleasure you can stand.

Chapter 14

QUESTIONS AND ANSWERS

———————————•———————————

Q. Who should be taken on the date first? The man or the woman?

A. Usually the woman should be taken on the date first. It will probably be different if the woman reads this book first and fears that her mate may resist too much if she tries to get him to read it. In that case you might just tell your husband that you are going to treat him to a very special "Date" and ask him to go along with you. After it is over, he will more than likely want more. That is the time to introduce your conditions for the second "date"— have him read up to Chapter 9 and apply all the instructions before the "date." You could also offer to be his

———————————•———————————

167

"coach" and read to him and fill in the blanks for him. Make it as easy as possible for both of you to win.

Remember, we men have very large and very, very fragile egos. It is important to let us know that there is nothing lacking or wrong with your sex life. Your sex life is great. *THE ONE HOUR ORGASM* is only about having more fun and more pleasure.

Q. Is there a down side to this method?

A. Yes! You can never go back to the way you were.

Q. What if we don't have an hour or the energy for a one hour session?

A. Good question and here is a great answer. It is called:

THE TWO MINUTE PLEASURE BREAK

Sometimes you really do not have an hour. At other times neither of you are in the mood to consider any long pleasuring session or the pressure of producing a result for yourself or your partner. Waiting too long to pleasure yourself is like not eating for a long period of time. You lose your appetite, but after even a small amount of food your appetite returns.

What if you only have a few minutes? If the most

you can nudge your partner into is a couple of minutes, a few minutes will be perfect.

Look at the clock and begin. Do whatever you can do, given your surroundings and resources. Try not to go anywhere without at least a small tube of your Vaseline and maybe even a couple of blankets in the trunk of your car.

At the end of the two minutes, ask if they want you to continue and for how long. With my wife, I was amazed at how much extra available time showed up at the end of just two minutes.

Even if you need to stop at the end of two minutes, it was two more than you would have had if you had not started. Also, you are peaking each other, building up the steam toward the "one hour" session.

Q. What if I ask to be "done" or to do my partner and they say no?

A. Don't take it personally or let it throw you. THE BASIC TRUTH TO WHY ANYONE SAYS "NO" TO ANY OFFER IS BECAUSE THEY PERCEIVE A LOSS. It is not the benefits they are saying no to, it is what they see as the down side to the offer.

So, if you make an offer to someone and the person rejects your offer, it is not you that is being rejected. It is your offer. If you want someone to say yes, make them a better offer. Find out or try to guess what part of the offer the person is afraid of or doesn't like. Ask if it is that particular part of the offer they are saying no to. Another possibility is that the offer may not have been good enough.

What if you offered to take someone out for a romantic dinner at McDonalds and they say no? What would happen if you upped your offer? Would they now say yes? How about going with you tonight to their favorite restaurant?

Q. What if my partner is so tumesced that they won't let me get close enough to detumesce them in any way?

A. The bottom line to handling resistance is to begin early. By the time either one of you are "tumesced" to the end of your rope, it is very difficult to bring up the idea of pleasure.

Beginning early is very poor advice if you have let each other go too long. The best answer I have found with my wife is to:

* be very compassionate,
* take all the blame and responsibility for having waited and anything else she can think of that she is disappointed in me for,
* ask what kind of punishment she thinks fit the crimes I have committed,
* and begin to put all of my attention on her.

Even if she wants me out of the room, I leave and keep thinking about her and what she would like next. From time to time I come back into the room to check on how she is feeling and ask if I can do this or that for her.

The main thing is that I keep showering her with my total attention. Remember, giving someone your full attention is the main ingredient for "detumescing" someone. It doesn't matter that they know what you are doing. It still works.

Q. Why can't I just "do" myself rather than having to worry about a relationship?

A. Of course you can, but you cannot cause yourself either pleasure or pain to the degree that someone else can who is doing the same thing to you.

Can you imagine twisting your own arm hard enough to make yourself reveal government secrets? Likewise, you cannot possibly give yourself the degree of pleasure that someone else can, especially when both of your attentions are on just you.

Q. What happens if somewhere along the line of growing and getting more pleasure, we run into some issue that we aren't able to figure out? What do we do then?

A. I am going to quote something that I took the liberty to rewrite slightly from the *I CHING*.

When something must be completed or a problem needs to be solved, often a struggle is inevitable. If the time for completing a transition arrives and one lacks the strength and the means for carrying it through, do not force it. Instead engage capable and reliable helpers, then make decisive steps.

In other words, get competent help. Dr. Robert Shaw, of the Family Institute of Berkeley, California, trains therapists in an advanced form of therapy skills. His students are taught effective therapy so they are capable of resolving problems in brief periods of time.

When I was in a training session that Dr. Shaw was teaching, I became aware of a level of technology in helping people that is available to all professionals and yet is only studied by some. If a therapist is committed to his clients, he needs to stay on the cutting edge of technology.

Q. If I am not careful, will I ever ruin her climax by peaking my partner too long?

A. Probably, but it is not important. The goal is pleasure. A climax, although desirable, is not necessary for pleasure. The good side of it is that if you do blow an orgasm for her, you have actually peaked her one more time. The next time you do her, she will really have a head of steam built up.

Q. I have a hard time accepting your premise that the woman is the source of sexual arousal.

A. So did I, but the more I checked it out, the clearer it became to me that it was so. The more I began to believe that my wife, Leah, was the source of my sexual arousal, the better my life became.

One day, while completing this book, I got up before 5 A.M. to complete a section I had been thinking about all night. I worked intensely all day, either on the book or in meetings. When I came to bed after midnight, my wife, Leah, was asleep. I got in bed and snuggled up close to her. All of a sudden I had an erection.

I looked around, but there was no one else there except the cat, so I figured it must be Leah. When I began to gently wake her up, she did not look too thrilled, but with a little persistence she came alive.

After it was over, she told me that she had been dreaming about sex and was very turned on in her dream. I, on the other hand, was at the end of a very long day and normally would have been sound asleep thirty seconds after my head hit the pillow.

I am so happy that I know who generates and transmits sexual energy. She is not always in touch with what she wants, but my little barometer never lies.

Q. Where do we go if we need more help?

A. If you get stuck and want help, there are many professionals around who earn their livelihoods by producing dynamic results helping couples to solve their relationship problems.

Q. Although we love what you say and get a lot of pleasure when we practice the techniques you have given us, we are finding ourselves putting off using the one hour orgasm method. It seems like we resist having pleasure.

A. HOW TO OVERCOME RESISTANCE.

Is there any area of your life where you feel you "should" want to do something or "should" know what to do?

Do you do it? Usually not.

I have found that when I am not doing something that I should be doing, it means that I need to get some help. This is especially true if I have been putting off doing whatever I have been avoiding for some unreasonable length of time.

I kept meaning to clean out the storage area in a warehouse that I had. Ten years later, after going through many upsets because I could not find something or had to buy another item to replace a lost one, I paid a group of people to help me. It was wonderful! In four hours we did what I had resisted doing, had been thinking about doing, had complained about not doing, and worried about for ten years.

This book will create more problems for you than you may be willing to figure out and overcome on your own. If you have followed the instructions in this book, you will have had a taste of what pleasure could be like. Begin to make pleasure a priority in your life.

If you are like me, you will be getting more work done in less time. Your relationships will be better and you will find that doing each other is a lot more fun than watching television reruns or most of the other things you were doing. Fortunately, you will be able to get all the pleasure you can stand out of a committed, monogamous, relationship.

The problem is that once you are committed to more pleasure in your life and your relationships, there is no turning back or standing still. You will need to continue to improve your skills and knowledge on a daily basis. You will probably resist doing this even though you know how much value you would get and how much fun you would have doing it.

YOUR PERSONAL INVITATION

Dr. Baranco and his staff do workshops on every phase of his work all across the country. If you would like a current schedule or more information to help you have more pleasure in your life and your relationship, send your request in a self addressed, stamped envelope to:

BREAKTHRU PUBLISHING
P.O.BOX 2866
HOUSTON, TEXAS 77252-2866

Please include your name and address and phone numbers if you want to be called.

Also, you can reach me by writing to the above address in care of Bob Schwartz. Please let us know how you are doing. Leah and I both are available for speaking engagements and guest appearances. Write us for more information.

After you have finished reading *THE ONE HOUR ORGASM*, you will probably have a lot of questions. Write them down and look for the answers as you read the book over and over again. Also, please send us a list of your questions and the problems you run into that slow you down. Send a self addressed-stamped envelope and we will put you on our mailing list. As new information is available we will let you know.

THE ONE HOUR ORGASM audio and video tapes will be available soon. Write to us if you would like to be on our mailing list. Also, if you would like a copy of *DIETS DON'T WORK* or the *DIETS DON'T WORK* double cassette audio tapes or the video tape, check with your local bookstore. If they are out of stock, you can order from us directly at the above address.

THE BEGINNING

This is a book that you will want to read over and over. Each time you read it you will increase the amount of fun and pleasure in your life. Turn to page 1 and begin now.